BUILDING YOUR DIGITAL **MARKETING EMPIRE**

Navigating Trends, Overcoming Challenges, and Achieving Success

Angela Dodson

ISBN: 978-1-7636914-0-7

Contents

CHAPTER 1:
The Rise of Digital Marketing

IN THE LAST two decades, the digital landscape has evolved at an unprecedented pace, transforming the way businesses operate and consumers interact. The rise of digital marketing has fundamentally changed the marketing paradigm, creating new opportunities and challenges for entrepreneurs and marketers alike. As we delve into the reasons behind this revolution, it becomes apparent why building a digital marketing empire is not just beneficial; it is becoming essential for success in today's economy.

The Evolution of Marketing

Historically, marketing relied on traditional methods such as print, radio, and television advertising. While these channels were effective in their time, they had limitations, including high costs, limited reach, and a lack of precise targeting. The advent of the internet in the late 20th century marked the beginning of a new era in marketing. With the rise of websites, search engines, and social media platforms, businesses gained access to a global audience at a fraction of the cost.

The introduction of digital marketing tools has allowed companies to employ data-driven strategies, enabling them to understand consumer behavior better and tailor their offerings accordingly. The digital marketing landscape includes a wide array of tactics, from content marketing and social media engagement to search engine optimization (SEO) and pay-per-click advertising. Each of these strategies provides unique ways to connect with potential customers, build brand awareness, and drive sales.

The Impact of Technology

Technological advancements have played a crucial role in the rise of digital marketing. The widespread use of smartphones, tablets, and high-speed internet has transformed the consumer experience. Today, consumers have access to information at their fingertips, allowing them to make informed purchasing decisions. For businesses, this means adapting to a more empowered consumer who expects personalized experiences and immediate responses.

Take the case of Nike, for instance. By leveraging technology, Nike has created a robust digital marketing strategy that includes a mobile app, personalized emails, and engaging social media content. The Nike app not only allows customers to purchase products but also offers personalized recommendations based on user behavior, fostering a deeper connection between the brand and its audience.

Changing Consumer Behavior

The shift towards digital marketing is also driven by changing consumer behavior. According to a report by Statista, over 4.6 billion people worldwide use the internet, with social media platforms witnessing significant growth. These platforms have become not just channels for communication but also powerful marketing tools. Consumers now spend a considerable amount of their time online, researching products, reading reviews, and engaging with brands.

This change in behavior has led to the rise of influencer marketing, where brands collaborate with social media influencers to reach specific demographics. For example, the beauty industry has seen a massive transformation with influencers like Huda Kattan and James Charles building empires through platforms like Instagram and YouTube. Their authenticity and relatability resonate with their followers, making them valuable partners for brands looking to penetrate the market.

Why Build a Digital Marketing Empire?

Given the undeniable advantages of digital marketing, it is clear why aspiring entrepreneurs should consider building a digital marketing empire. Here are several compelling reasons:

1. **Lower Barriers to Entry**: Traditional marketing methods often require significant financial investment, making it challenging for small businesses to compete. In contrast, digital marketing offers cost-effective strategies that allow

even startups to establish a presence. Platforms like social media and email marketing can be utilized with minimal budgets, enabling entrepreneurs to reach their target audience without breaking the bank.

2. **Global Reach**: Digital marketing transcends geographical boundaries. With an online presence, businesses can access a global audience, expanding their market potential exponentially. For example, an artisan selling handmade jewelry can reach customers from different countries through an eCommerce website, thereby increasing sales opportunities beyond local markets.
3. **Data-Driven Decisions**: Digital marketing provides access to valuable data and analytics tools that help businesses measure the effectiveness of their campaigns. By analyzing metrics such as website traffic, conversion rates, and customer engagement, entrepreneurs can make informed decisions to optimize their marketing strategies. This data-driven approach allows for continuous improvement and better allocation of resources.
4. **Flexibility and Adaptability:** The digital landscape is dynamic, with trends and technologies evolving rapidly. Digital marketing allows businesses to be agile, quickly adapting their strategies based on market changes or consumer feedback. For instance, during the COVID-19 pandemic, many companies pivoted to online sales and

virtual experiences to maintain customer engagement, showcasing the flexibility of digital marketing.

5. **Building Relationships**: Digital marketing is not just about transactions; it is about building relationships with customers. Through engaging content, personalized communication, and responsive customer service, businesses can foster loyalty and trust. Brands like Starbucks have mastered this by creating a community through their rewards program and social media interactions, encouraging repeat business and customer advocacy.

Case Study: Airbnb

Airbnb stands as a prime example of a company that has built a digital marketing empire through innovative strategies. Launched in 2008, Airbnb leveraged the power of digital platforms to create a unique marketplace for travelers seeking affordable accommodations. By focusing on user-generated content, reviews, and social media engagement, Airbnb rapidly gained traction.

The company's marketing strategy emphasizes storytelling, showcasing authentic experiences shared by users. Their campaigns, such as "Live There," encourage travelers to immerse themselves in local cultures, appealing to a growing segment of consumers seeking unique travel experiences. Airbnb's success illustrates how a strong digital marketing strategy can disrupt traditional industries and create a powerful brand presence.

As we have explored in this chapter, the rise of digital

marketing has reshaped the business landscape, offering unprecedented opportunities for entrepreneurs. The combination of technological advancements, changing consumer behaviors, and the potential for global reach makes building a digital marketing empire an attractive prospect.

In the following chapters, we will dive deeper into the practical steps you can take to leverage these opportunities, create in-demand digital products, and establish your own successful digital marketing business. The journey may be challenging, but with the right knowledge and strategies, you can build a thriving empire in the digital realm. Let's embark on this exciting journey together!

CHAPTER 2: Understanding Digital Products

IN A WORLD increasingly driven by digital interactions, understanding digital products is crucial for anyone looking to build a successful digital marketing empire. Digital products offer unique advantages over traditional physical products, providing entrepreneurs with opportunities to create, distribute, and monetize offerings in innovative ways. This chapter will explore the definition and types of digital products, the benefits of selling them, and current market trends and consumer demand.

Definition and Types of Digital Products

Digital products are intangible goods that can be sold and delivered online. Unlike physical products that require manufacturing, storage, and shipping, digital products are typically created once and can be sold an unlimited number of times. This scalability is one of the primary reasons entrepreneurs are drawn to digital products.

Types of Digital Products:

1. **E-books:** These are digital versions of books that can be read on computers, tablets, or e-readers. E-books are popular due to their accessibility and the ease with which they can be distributed. Authors can self-publish on platforms like Amazon Kindle Direct Publishing or sell directly through their websites. For instance, best-selling author Tim Ferriss has successfully leveraged e-books to build his brand and reach millions of readers.
2. **Online Courses:** The e-learning industry is booming, with online courses becoming a preferred method for people seeking to learn new skills or gain knowledge. Platforms like Udemy, Teachable, and Coursera enable creators to design and sell courses on various topics. For example, Marie Forleo has built a multi-million dollar business by offering online courses that empower entrepreneurs to build their brands.
3. **Membership Sites:** These platforms provide exclusive content, resources, and community access to subscribers who pay a recurring fee. Membership sites can cover various niches, from fitness and personal development to business and finance. An example is the site "The Membership Guys," which offers resources and support for those looking to create their own membership websites.
4. **Digital Downloads:** These include templates, stock photos, graphics, music, and software that customers can

download after purchase. Websites like Etsy and Creative Market specialize in selling digital downloads, allowing creators to monetize their skills. For instance, designers can sell website templates or graphics, while musicians can offer royalty-free music for use in videos.

5. **Apps and Software:** Mobile applications and software solutions are also digital products. They can solve specific problems or provide entertainment. Companies like Slack and Zoom have gained immense popularity by offering software that enhances productivity and communication. Entrepreneurs can create apps that cater to niche markets, offering tailored solutions.
6. **Webinars and Live Events:** While often considered a part of content marketing, webinars and live events can also be classified as digital products. They allow businesses to engage with their audience in real-time, providing valuable information while promoting products or services. Many marketers use platforms like Zoom or WebinarJam to host these events, generating leads and sales.
7. **Podcasts:** With the rise of audio content, podcasts have become a significant digital product. Entrepreneurs can monetize podcasts through sponsorships, listener donations, or premium content subscriptions. Joe Rogan's podcast, for example, has turned into a multi-million dollar venture, showcasing the potential of audio content.

The Benefits of Selling Digital Products

Selling digital products comes with a multitude of advantages that make them an attractive option for entrepreneurs.

8. **Low Overhead Costs**: One of the most significant benefits of digital products is the low overhead. There are no manufacturing, storage, or shipping costs involved. Once a digital product is created, it can be sold repeatedly without the associated costs of physical goods. This allows entrepreneurs to focus their resources on marketing and product development.
9. **Scalability**: Digital products can be scaled easily. Unlike physical products that require additional resources for each unit sold, digital products can be delivered to an unlimited number of customers without any additional effort. This scalability allows entrepreneurs to maximize their profits without increasing their workload.
10. **Global Reach**: With digital products, businesses can access a global market. An entrepreneur in one country can sell their products to customers worldwide without geographical limitations. This broad reach opens up numerous opportunities for growth and diversification, allowing businesses to tap into various markets.
11. **Recurring Revenue Potential**: Many digital product models, such as subscription services or membership sites, offer the potential for recurring revenue. This predictable income stream can provide financial stability and allow

entrepreneurs to invest in further growth. For example, platforms like Netflix and Spotify generate substantial recurring revenue through their subscription models.

12. **Flexibility and Convenience:** Digital products can be created, distributed, and updated quickly. Entrepreneurs can respond to market trends and consumer feedback in real-time, allowing them to stay relevant. Furthermore, customers appreciate the convenience of accessing digital products instantly, whether they are e-books, courses, or software.
13. **Environmentally Friendly:** As digital products do not require physical materials or shipping, they are a more sustainable option compared to traditional products. As consumers become more environmentally conscious, offering digital products can align with their values and preferences.
14. **Diverse Revenue Streams:** Entrepreneurs can create multiple digital products across various niches, diversifying their income sources. For instance, a business coach might offer e-books, online courses, and membership sites, reducing reliance on a single product and increasing overall revenue potential.

Market Trends and Consumer Demand

Understanding market trends and consumer demand is critical for anyone looking to succeed in selling digital products. Here are several key trends shaping the landscape:

15. **The Growth of E-Learning:** The e-learning industry has seen exponential growth, especially in recent years. According to a report by Global Market Insights, the e-learning market is expected to reach $375 billion by 2026. This growth is driven by the increasing demand for online education and the convenience of learning from home. Entrepreneurs can capitalize on this trend by creating online courses or educational resources that cater to specific audiences.
16. **Personalization and Customization:** Consumers increasingly seek personalized experiences. Digital products that allow for customization—such as personalized fitness plans, tailored coaching sessions, or bespoke digital downloads—are gaining popularity. Businesses that offer tailored solutions can foster stronger connections with their customers and enhance loyalty.
17. **Subscription Models:** Subscription-based services continue to thrive, with consumers appreciating the convenience and value they provide. Whether it's streaming services, software, or educational platforms, subscriptions offer ongoing engagement and recurring revenue for entrepreneurs. For example, platforms like

Skillshare and MasterClass have successfully harnessed this trend by providing a library of courses for a monthly fee.

18. **Mobile Optimization:** As smartphones and mobile devices become ubiquitous, optimizing digital products for mobile use is essential. Consumers increasingly access content on their mobile devices, so ensuring that e-books, courses, and websites are mobile-friendly is crucial. Entrepreneurs should prioritize mobile design to reach a broader audience effectively.
19. **Social Media Influence:** Social media platforms play a significant role in shaping consumer behavior and preferences. Marketers leverage platforms like Instagram, TikTok, and YouTube to promote digital products and engage with their audiences. Collaborating with influencers can amplify reach and credibility, making social media an essential tool for digital product marketing.
20. **Increased Value for Free Content:** Consumers are bombarded with information and content daily. As a result, offering valuable free content can help build trust and establish authority in a niche. Entrepreneurs can provide free resources, such as e-books, webinars, or guides, to attract potential customers and lead them toward purchasing premium products.
21. **Focus on Mental Health and Wellness:** The growing awareness of mental health and well-being has led

to increased demand for products that address these concerns. Digital products related to mindfulness, stress management, and personal development are gaining traction. Entrepreneurs can create courses, e-books, or apps that cater to this growing market segment.

Case Studies: Success Stories in Digital Products

To illustrate the potential of digital products, let's explore a few success stories of entrepreneurs who have built thriving businesses around them.

Case Study 1: Pat Flynn

Pat Flynn is a prime example of how digital products can transform an individual's career. After losing his job in architecture, he turned to online business and created the popular website Smart Passive Income. Through a combination of e-books, online courses, and affiliate marketing, Flynn built a multi-million dollar empire. His flagship course, "Power-Up Podcasting," teaches aspiring podcasters how to launch and grow their shows, demonstrating the demand for quality education in the digital space.

Case Study 2: Amy Porterfield

Amy Porterfield is a leading expert in online course creation and digital marketing. She built her business by launching the course "List Builder's Lab," which teaches entrepreneurs how to grow their email lists. Porterfield's success stems from her ability to provide valuable content and practical strategies, leading to a loyal following. She has since expanded her offerings, including additional courses and a successful podcast, further establishing her brand in the digital marketing space.

Case Study 3: Canva

Canva, the graphic design platform, has revolutionized the way individuals and businesses create visual content. Founded in 2013, Canva offers a suite of digital products, including design templates, images, and tools for creating professional graphics. By focusing on user-friendliness and accessibility, Canva has attracted millions of users and generated substantial revenue through its subscription model. The platform exemplifies how digital products can disrupt traditional industries and empower users.

Practical Advice for Entrepreneurs

As you consider entering the world of digital products, here are some practical tips to guide your journey:

1. **Identify Your Niche**: Conduct thorough market research to identify areas where you can provide value. Look for gaps in the market or underserved audiences, and tailor your digital products to meet their needs.
2. **Create High-Quality Products**: Quality matters. Invest time and effort into creating valuable digital products

that resonate with your audience. Whether it's an online course, e-book, or software, ensure that your offerings are well-designed, informative, and user-friendly.

3. **Leverage Feedback:** Use customer feedback to refine your products and marketing strategies. Encourage reviews and testimonials, and be open to making adjustments based on user experiences.
4. **Invest in Marketing:** Once your digital products are ready, dedicate resources to marketing them effectively. Utilize social media, content marketing, and email campaigns to reach your target audience. Consider collaborating with influencers to amplify your reach.
5. **Stay Current:** The digital landscape is constantly evolving. Stay informed about market trends, consumer preferences, and technological advancements to remain competitive. Attend webinars, read industry blogs, and engage with communities to keep your knowledge up to date.
6. **Build a Community:** Foster a sense of community around your digital products. Engage with your audience through social media, forums, or membership sites. Building relationships with customers can enhance loyalty and lead to repeat business.
7. **Diversify Your Offerings:** Consider creating multiple digital products within your niche to diversify your income streams. This could involve developing complementary

products, such as e-books alongside online courses or offering different pricing tiers for your services.

Understanding digital products is essential for anyone looking to build a digital marketing empire. Their scalability, low overhead costs, and global reach make them an attractive option for entrepreneurs. By exploring various types of digital products, recognizing the benefits they offer, and staying attuned to market trends, you can position yourself for success.

As you embark on your journey in the digital marketplace, remember that quality, creativity, and customer engagement are key to standing out in a competitive landscape. In the following chapters, we will explore practical strategies for creating and marketing your digital products, empowering you to build a thriving business in the digital realm. Let's take the next steps together!

CHAPTER 3:
Finding Your Niche

IN THE VAST and competitive landscape of digital marketing, finding your niche is one of the most critical steps you can take toward building a successful business. A well-defined niche not only helps you stand out from the competition but also allows you to target your audience more effectively, ensuring that your marketing efforts resonate with those most likely to engage with your products. This chapter will guide you through the process of identifying your passion and expertise, conducting market research, and analyzing competitors to carve out your unique space in the digital marketplace.

Identifying Your Passion and Expertise

Finding your niche starts with introspection. Identifying what you are passionate about and where your expertise lies is crucial for several reasons:

1. **Sustained Motivation:** Building a digital marketing empire takes time and effort. When you are passionate about your niche, you are more likely to stay motivated, even when faced with challenges. Your enthusiasm will translate into your work, making it more enjoyable and authentic.
2. **Authenticity:** Consumers are drawn to authenticity. When you are knowledgeable about your niche, you can create valuable content that resonates with your audience. Your genuine interest will shine through, building trust and credibility.
3. **Expertise Advantage:** Leveraging your existing skills and knowledge can give you a competitive edge. If you already have experience in a particular area, you can create products or services that reflect your expertise, reducing the learning curve and increasing your chances of success.

Steps to Identify Your Passion and Expertise:

4. **Self-Reflection:** Take time to reflect on your interests, hobbies, and skills. What topics excite you? What activities do you enjoy doing in your free time? Make a list of these interests and consider how they could translate into a digital product or service.
5. **Evaluate Your Skills:** Assess your skills and experience. What are you good at? Think about your professional background, education, and any specialized training you

have received. Identify areas where you can leverage your expertise to create value for others.

6. **Seek Feedback:** Sometimes, others can see strengths in us that we may overlook. Ask friends, family, or colleagues about your strengths and what they believe you are passionate about. Their insights may help you identify potential niches.
7. **Consider Trends:** While passion and expertise are crucial, it's also essential to consider market trends. Are there emerging topics or industries gaining popularity? Aligning your passions with current trends can enhance your chances of success.

Case Study: Marie Forleo

Marie Forleo is a prime example of someone who successfully identified her passion and expertise. Initially starting her career in the fitness industry, she recognized her love for entrepreneurship and personal development. By combining her passions, she created a digital platform that offers online courses, coaching, and content focused on helping individuals build their businesses. Forleo's journey illustrates the power of aligning passion with expertise to create a thriving online presence.

Conducting Market Research

Once you have identified potential niches based on your passions and expertise, the next step is conducting thorough market research. Market research helps you understand your target audience, the demand for your products, and the competitive landscape. Here are the key components of effective market research:

1. **Define Your Target Audience**: Understanding who your ideal customers are is essential for tailoring your products and marketing efforts. Consider demographics such as age, gender, location, income level, and interests. Creating buyer personas can help you visualize your audience and their needs.
2. **Identify Pain Points**: Determine the challenges your target audience faces within your niche. What problems are they trying to solve? Conduct surveys, interviews, or engage with online communities to gain insights into their pain points. Addressing these issues will allow you to create products that genuinely resonate with your audience.
3. **Analyze Demand**: Assess the demand for your potential niche by exploring search trends, social media discussions, and industry reports. Tools like Google Trends, SEMrush, or Ahrefs can help you identify keywords and topics that are gaining traction. Understanding the

demand will guide you in choosing a niche with growth potential.

4. **Use Social Media**: Social media platforms are treasure troves of information. Join relevant groups, forums, or communities where your target audience hangs out. Pay attention to the questions they ask, the content they share, and the challenges they discuss. This real-time feedback can provide valuable insights into market needs.
5. **Explore Online Resources**: Utilize online resources to gather data about your niche. Websites like Statista, Pew Research, and industry-specific blogs often provide reports and statistics that can inform your understanding of market trends and consumer behavior.

Example of Market Research: Health and Wellness Niche

Suppose you are passionate about health and wellness. To conduct market research, you would start by defining your target audience—perhaps busy professionals aged 25-40 who seek convenient ways to maintain a healthy lifestyle. Next, identify their pain points, such as lack of time for meal prep or difficulty finding effective workout solutions. By analyzing search trends, you may discover that topics like "quick healthy meals" and "home workout routines" are gaining traction. Engaging in health and wellness communities on social media could provide further insights into the specific needs of your audience.

Analyzing Competitors

Understanding your competitors is a vital component of finding your niche. Analyzing their strengths and weaknesses will help you identify opportunities and differentiate yourself in the market. Here's how to conduct a thorough competitor analysis:

1. **Identify Your Competitors**: Start by identifying your direct and indirect competitors within your niche. Direct competitors offer similar products or services, while indirect competitors address the same audience but may provide alternative solutions.
2. **Assess Their Offerings**: Take a close look at your competitors' products, pricing, and marketing strategies. What types of digital products are they offering? How do they position themselves in the market? Analyze their strengths, weaknesses, and unique selling propositions (USPs).
3. **Evaluate Their Online Presence**: Review your competitors' online presence, including their websites and social media profiles. Pay attention to their content strategy, engagement levels, and customer reviews. Tools like SimilarWeb or BuzzSumo can provide insights into their website traffic and content performance.
4. **Learn from Their Successes and Failures**: Analyze what works well for your competitors and what doesn't. By studying successful campaigns, you can gain inspiration for your strategies. Conversely, identifying their

weaknesses allows you to position yourself as a better alternative.

5. **Find Your Unique Selling Proposition (USP)**: After analyzing competitors, determine how you can differentiate yourself. What unique value can you offer? This could be in the form of a unique product feature, exceptional customer service, or a different pricing model. Your USP will help you stand out in a crowded market.

Case Study: Headspace vs. Calm

Headspace and Calm are two leading apps in the mindfulness and meditation space. Both offer similar services, yet they have carved out their unique niches. Headspace focuses on providing guided meditation with a light-hearted and animated approach, appealing to a younger audience. Calm, on the other hand, emphasizes relaxation and sleep, featuring soothing sounds and nature visuals. By analyzing their offerings and marketing strategies, you can see how both companies have successfully differentiated themselves within the same market.

Practical Advice for Finding Your Niche

As you embark on the journey of finding your niche, consider the following practical advice:

1. **Start Small**: Don't feel pressured to choose an overly broad niche. Starting with a specific sub-niche allows you

to focus your efforts and establish authority more easily. Once you gain traction, you can expand your offerings.

2. **Test Your Ideas:** Before fully committing to a niche, consider testing your ideas through pilot projects or minimum viable products (MVPs). Create a simple version of your digital product and gather feedback from your target audience. This approach will help you validate your niche and refine your offerings.
3. **Engage with Your Audience:** Building relationships with your audience is critical. Use social media, email newsletters, and online communities to engage with potential customers. Ask for their opinions, conduct polls, and encourage discussions. This interaction will provide valuable insights into their needs and preferences.
4. **Stay Adaptable:** The digital landscape is ever-evolving. Be open to adjusting your niche or offerings based on market trends and consumer feedback. Flexibility is key to long-term success in digital marketing.
5. **Invest in Continuous Learning:** The more you learn about your niche, the better equipped you'll be to serve your audience. Read industry-related books, attend webinars, and participate in relevant courses. Staying informed about developments in your niche will enhance your credibility.

Finding your niche is a fundamental step in building a successful digital marketing empire. By identifying your passion and expertise, conducting thorough market research, and analyzing competitors, you can carve out a unique space in the digital marketplace. Your niche will not only define your target audience but also guide your product development and marketing strategies.

As you move forward, remember that the journey of finding your niche is an ongoing process. Stay engaged with your audience, adapt to changing trends, and continuously refine your offerings. In the next chapters, we will explore strategies for creating high-quality digital products that cater to your niche and effectively market them to your target audience.

CHAPTER 4: Creating High-Quality Digital Products

IN THE REALM of digital marketing, creating high-quality digital products is paramount to your success. Quality products not only attract customers but also foster trust and loyalty, leading to sustained growth in your digital marketing empire. This chapter will explore the various types of digital products you can create, including e-books, online courses, membership sites, and digital downloads. We will also discuss the tools and resources available for product creation, along with tips for ensuring quality and value in your offerings.

Types of Digital Products to Consider

Digital products come in several forms, each with its own unique advantages and target audiences. Understanding the types of digital products you can create will help you align your offerings with your expertise and the needs of your audience.

E-books have become a popular choice for many entrepreneurs looking to share their knowledge and expertise. These digital books can cover a wide range of topics, from how-to guides and self-help books to comprehensive industry analyses. The beauty of e-books lies in their accessibility; they can be easily distributed through various platforms like Amazon Kindle, Apple Books, or directly from your website. E-books also require relatively low production costs, making them an attractive option for those starting their digital product journey.

When creating an e-book, it's essential to focus on providing value to your readers. A well-researched, informative, and engaging e-book can establish you as an authority in your niche. For instance, if you're a fitness expert, writing an e-book on "30-Day Meal Plans for Busy Professionals" can attract a specific audience looking for actionable advice.

Online courses are another lucrative option in the digital product arena. The e-learning industry has exploded in recent years, with more people seeking to acquire new skills from the comfort of their homes. Online courses can vary in length and format, including video lessons, quizzes, and downloadable resources. Platforms like Udemy, Teachable, and Kajabi make it easy to create and sell your courses, allowing you to reach a global audience.

The key to a successful online course is to ensure that it addresses a specific problem or need. For example, if you're a social media marketer, you could create a course on "Mastering Instagram for Small Businesses." By providing practical tips, real-life examples, and actionable steps, you can help your students achieve tangible results, enhancing their learning experience.

Membership sites offer a unique way to generate recurring revenue while providing ongoing value to your audience. These platforms grant subscribers access to exclusive content, resources, and community interaction for a monthly or annual fee. Membership sites can cover various topics, from personal finance and business development to fitness and wellness.

To create a successful membership site, it's crucial to consistently provide fresh and valuable content. This could include monthly webinars, downloadable resources, community forums, or one-on-one coaching sessions. For example, the "Fizzle" membership site focuses on helping entrepreneurs build sustainable businesses, offering a wealth of resources, training, and a supportive community.

Digital downloads, such as templates, graphics, and stock photos, are another excellent option for creators. These products can be quickly produced and easily sold, making them highly scalable. Platforms like Etsy, Creative Market, and Gumroad allow you to showcase and sell your digital downloads to a broad audience.

For instance, if you're a graphic designer, you could create and sell social media templates for entrepreneurs looking to enhance their online presence. By offering high-quality, visually appealing designs, you can attract customers who are willing to pay for your expertise.

Tools and Resources for Creation

Creating high-quality digital products requires the right tools and resources. Fortunately, there are many options available to help streamline the process and ensure your products meet professional standards.

For e-books, tools like Scrivener and Google Docs can help you organize your content and streamline the writing process. Scrivener is particularly useful for larger projects, as it allows you to break your work into manageable sections and easily rearrange them as needed. Once your e-book is complete, you can use design software like Adobe InDesign or Canva to create an eye-catching layout and cover design.

When it comes to online courses, platforms like Teachable and Thinkific provide user-friendly interfaces for creating and selling your courses. They offer built-in features, such as video hosting, quizzes, and progress tracking, which can enhance the learning experience for your students. For video creation, tools like Camtasia or ScreenFlow allow you to record and edit professional-quality videos, while platforms like Zoom can facilitate live sessions.

Membership sites can be built using platforms like MemberPress or Kajabi, which provide comprehensive solutions for managing subscriptions, content, and community interactions. These tools often include features like drip content, member forums, and email marketing integration, making it easier to engage with your audience.

For digital downloads, platforms like Gumroad or Sellfy allow you to set up an online store to showcase your products. These services handle payment processing and file delivery, allowing you to focus on creating and marketing your products. Additionally, design tools like Canva, Adobe Illustrator, or Affinity Designer can help you create professional-looking templates and graphics.

Tips for Ensuring Quality and Value

Creating high-quality digital products is essential for building trust and establishing your brand in the market. Here are some tips to ensure your products provide value to your audience:

Focus on Research: Thoroughly research your chosen topic to ensure that your content is accurate, up-to-date, and comprehensive. Utilize reputable sources, conduct interviews with experts, and gather case studies to support your claims. Delivering well-researched information will enhance your credibility and authority in your niche.

Know Your Audience: Understanding your target audience is crucial for creating products that resonate with them. Conduct surveys, engage with your audience on social media, and seek feedback to identify their needs and preferences. Tailor your content to address their pain points and provide solutions.

Invest in Professional Design: The visual appeal of your digital products can greatly influence their perceived value. Invest time in creating an attractive layout, cover design, and graphics. If design isn't your strong suit, consider hiring a freelance designer to ensure your products look professional.

Create Engaging Content: Whether it's an e-book, online

course, or membership site, make your content engaging and interactive. Use storytelling techniques, visuals, and real-life examples to captivate your audience. Break up lengthy text with images, bullet points, and headings to enhance readability.

Test and Revise: Before launching your digital product, seek feedback from a small group of beta testers. Their insights can help you identify areas for improvement and ensure that your product meets the expectations of your target audience. Be open to making revisions and iterating on your content.

Offer Extras: Enhance the value of your digital products by including bonus materials or additional resources. For example, if you're selling an online course, consider providing downloadable worksheets, templates, or access to a private community. These extras can increase the perceived value and encourage customers to invest in your offerings.

Stay Current: The digital landscape is constantly evolving, and it's essential to stay updated on industry trends and best practices. Regularly revise and refresh your content to ensure it remains relevant and valuable to your audience. This commitment to quality will help you build a loyal customer base.

Case Studies: Successful Digital Product Creators

To further illustrate the principles of creating high-quality digital products, let's take a look at a few successful creators who have made their mark in the digital space.

Case Study: Amy Porterfield

Amy Porterfield is a leading expert in online course creation and digital marketing. Her signature course, "Digital Course Academy," teaches entrepreneurs how to create and sell their own online courses. Porterfield's success can be attributed to her ability to provide immense value to her audience.

She conducts thorough research to understand her target audience's pain points and needs. By offering real-life examples, actionable steps, and engaging content, Porterfield has built a loyal following. Her commitment to quality is evident in her beautifully designed course materials and professional production quality in her videos.

Case Study: Tim Ferriss

Tim Ferriss, author of "The 4-Hour Workweek," has successfully leveraged digital products to build his brand. Alongside his best-selling books, Ferriss offers online courses and resources that delve deeper into the concepts he discusses in his books.

His course, "The 4-Hour Chef," combines cooking with productivity tips, demonstrating Ferriss's unique approach to learning. By offering a mix of valuable content, engaging visuals, and interactive elements, Ferriss has created a high-quality digital product that resonates with his audience.

Case Study: Canva (I know we discussed it earlier, but it's such a great example let's look at it a little more)

Canva, the graphic design platform, has revolutionized the way individuals and businesses create visual content. While Canva itself is a digital product, the company also offers extensive resources, including tutorials, templates, and design courses.

Canva's commitment to quality is evident in its user-friendly interface, extensive library of design elements, and educational resources. By continuously updating its offerings and providing valuable content, Canva has established itself as a go-to platform for design needs.

Creating high-quality digital products is essential for building a successful digital marketing empire. By understanding the different types of digital products, utilizing the right tools and resources, and ensuring quality and value, you can create offerings that resonate with your audience and establish your authority in your niche.

As you embark on your journey to create digital products, remember that the process may take time and effort. However, the rewards of building a loyal customer base, generating income, and establishing your brand will be well worth it. In the following chapters, we will explore effective marketing strategies to promote your digital products and reach your target audience, helping you to maximize your impact in the digital marketplace. Let's continue this exciting journey together!

CHAPTER 5:
Building Your Brand

IN THE DIGITAL marketplace, building a strong and memorable brand is essential for standing out in a crowded field. A well-defined brand not only attracts customers but also fosters loyalty and trust, ultimately leading to sustained business growth. This chapter will explore how to create a memorable brand identity, develop a unique selling proposition (USP), and craft a compelling brand story that resonates with your audience.

Creating a Memorable Brand Identity

Brand identity encompasses all the elements that define how your business is perceived by consumers. It includes your logo, color palette, typography, voice, and overall aesthetic. A memorable brand identity is crucial for differentiating your business from competitors and creating a lasting impression on your target audience.

The first step in creating your brand identity is to understand your target audience. Who are they? What are their preferences, values, and pain points? Conducting thorough market research will help you gain insights into what resonates with your audience. This understanding will guide your decisions as you develop your brand identity.

Next, consider the emotional response you want to evoke in your audience. What feelings do you want your brand to inspire? Whether it's trust, excitement, comfort, or empowerment, the emotional connection you establish will play a significant role in how your audience perceives your brand.

Once you have a clear understanding of your audience and the emotions you want to evoke, you can start designing your brand elements. Your logo is often the first visual representation of your brand that customers encounter, so it's essential to create a logo that reflects your brand's personality and values. For instance, a tech startup might choose a modern, sleek logo, while a wellness brand may opt for softer, organic shapes and colors.

Color plays a crucial role in brand identity, as different colors evoke different emotions. For example, blue is often associated with trust and professionalism, while green conveys growth and health. Choose a color palette that aligns with your brand's personality and resonates with your audience. Consistency in color usage across all branding materials helps reinforce brand recognition.

Typography also contributes to your brand identity. The fonts you choose should reflect your brand's character. A playful brand might use whimsical fonts, while a luxury brand may opt for elegant, serif fonts. Ensure that your typography is legible and complements your overall design.

The voice of your brand is another critical aspect of your identity. Your tone should be consistent across all platforms, whether it's your website, social media, or email communications. Are you formal or casual? Inspirational or informative? Your brand voice should resonate with your target audience and reflect your brand's personality.

Once you have developed your brand identity, it's essential to implement it consistently across all touchpoints. This includes your website, social media profiles, marketing materials, and customer interactions. Consistency helps build recognition and trust, making it easier for customers to connect with your brand.

Case Study: Airbnb

Airbnb is a prime example of a brand that has successfully created a memorable identity. The company's logo, a simple yet recognizable symbol known as the "Bélo," represents belonging and community. Airbnb's color palette is warm and inviting, reflecting the feeling of home that the brand aims to promote.

Airbnb's brand voice is friendly, inclusive, and approachable. Their messaging often emphasizes the unique experiences that come from staying in local homes rather than traditional hotels. By maintaining a consistent brand identity across their website, app, and marketing materials, Airbnb has established itself as a trusted and recognizable brand in the travel industry.

Developing a Unique Selling Proposition (USP)

Your unique selling proposition (USP) is what sets your business apart from competitors. It defines the unique value that your product or service offers and answers the question: "Why should customers choose you over others?" A well-defined USP is essential for attracting and retaining customers in a competitive market.

To develop your USP, start by analyzing your competitors. What are their strengths and weaknesses? What do they offer, and where do they fall short? Understanding the competitive landscape will help you identify opportunities to differentiate yourself.

Next, reflect on your own offerings. What unique features or benefits does your product provide? This could be anything from superior quality, innovative design, exceptional customer service, or a niche focus. For example, if you're selling online courses, your USP might be that your courses include personalized feedback and coaching sessions, which is not commonly offered by competitors.

Consider the specific needs and pain points of your target audience. How does your product address their challenges better than others? By aligning your USP with the needs of your audience, you can create a compelling case for why they should choose your brand.

Once you have defined your USP, it's essential to communicate it clearly and consistently across all marketing channels. This includes your website, social media, advertising, and email campaigns. Use concise and impactful messaging that highlights the unique benefits of your offerings.

Case Study: TOMS Shoes

TOMS Shoes is an excellent example of a brand that has successfully developed a strong USP. The company's mission to provide a pair of shoes to a child in need for every pair sold sets it apart from competitors. This "One for One" model resonates deeply with socially conscious consumers who want to make a positive impact with their purchases.

TOMS effectively communicates its USP through its marketing campaigns, emphasizing the positive social change that customers contribute to by buying their products. This commitment to social responsibility has helped TOMS build a loyal customer base and establish itself as a recognizable brand in the footwear industry.

Crafting a Compelling Brand Story

A compelling brand story is an essential component of your brand identity. It goes beyond just the facts of your business; it encompasses the values, mission, and vision that drive your brand. A well-crafted story connects with your audience on an emotional level, helping them relate to your brand and feel invested in its success.

To create your brand story, begin by reflecting on the origin of your business. What inspired you to start it? What challenges have you faced along the way? Sharing your journey, including your motivations and experiences, can create authenticity and relatability.

Next, consider the mission and values that define your brand. What do you stand for, and what principles guide your business decisions? Communicating these values in your brand story helps establish a connection with customers who share similar beliefs. For example, if your brand is committed to sustainability, highlight your eco-friendly practices in your story.

Your brand story should also convey the impact you aim to make in your industry or community. What change do you hope to bring about through your products or services? By articulating your vision, you can inspire customers to join you on your journey and become advocates for your brand.

When sharing your brand story, consider incorporating various formats. This could include written content on your website, engaging videos, social media posts, or blog articles. Visual storytelling, such as behind-the-scenes footage or customer testimonials, can also enhance your narrative.

It's essential to weave your brand story throughout all aspects of your marketing, from your website copy to your social media posts. Consistency in storytelling reinforces your brand identity and helps create a cohesive narrative that resonates with your audience.

Case Study: Warby Parker

Warby Parker, an eyewear company, has built its brand around a compelling story of accessibility and social responsibility. The founders started Warby Parker to disrupt the eyewear industry, which they felt was overpriced and inaccessible. Their mission to provide affordable, stylish eyewear while giving back to the community has been central to their brand narrative.

Warby Parker shares its story through engaging content that highlights its commitment to social impact. For every pair of glasses sold, the company donates a pair to someone in need. This story resonates with socially-conscious consumers, fostering a sense of community and purpose around the brand.

Practical Advice for Building Your Brand

As you embark on the journey of building your brand, consider the following practical tips:

Focus on Authenticity: Authenticity is key to building trust with your audience. Be transparent about your values, mission, and challenges. Share your journey and experiences to create a genuine connection with your customers.

Engage with Your Audience: Building a brand is a two-way street. Engage with your audience through social media, email newsletters, and community forums. Encourage feedback and listen to their needs. By fostering a sense of community, you can strengthen brand loyalty.

Invest in Quality Design: Your brand identity should reflect your commitment to quality. Invest in professional design services for your logo, website, and marketing materials. A polished and cohesive visual identity enhances your brand's credibility.

Stay Consistent: Consistency is crucial for brand recognition. Ensure that your branding elements, messaging, and tone remain consistent across all platforms. This consistency reinforces your brand identity and makes it easier for customers to connect with you.

Adapt and Evolve: The digital landscape is constantly changing, and so are consumer preferences. Stay informed about market trends and be willing to adapt your brand strategy as needed. Continuously evaluate your brand's performance and make adjustments to stay relevant.

Tell Your Story: Your brand story is a powerful tool for connecting with your audience. Share your journey, values, and mission in a way that resonates with your customers. Use storytelling techniques to make your narrative engaging and relatable.

Monitor Your Brand Reputation: Pay attention to how your brand is perceived online. Monitor social media mentions, customer reviews, and feedback. Address any concerns promptly and maintain an open line of communication with your audience.

Building a strong and memorable brand is essential for thriving in the digital marketplace. By creating a compelling brand identity, developing a unique selling proposition, and crafting a captivating brand story, you can establish a brand that resonates with your audience and stands out from the competition.

As you move forward, remember that building a brand is

an ongoing process. Stay engaged with your audience, adapt to changing trends, and continuously refine your brand strategy. In the upcoming chapters, we will delve into effective marketing strategies to promote your digital products and reach your target audience, helping you maximize your impact in the digital realm.

CHAPTER 6: Setting Up Your Online Presence

In today's digital age, establishing a robust online presence is crucial for the success of any digital marketing venture. Whether you are selling digital products, offering services, or building a brand, your online presence is often the first point of contact between you and your potential customers. This chapter will guide you through the essential steps for setting up your online presence, including choosing the right platform, creating essential pages for your digital business, and optimizing for search engines (SEO).

Choosing the Right Platform

The first step in establishing your online presence is selecting the right platform. The platform you choose will determine how you present your products or services, engage with your audience, and conduct transactions. There are various options available, each with its unique features and benefits.

When considering your options, it's essential to align the platform with your business goals and target audience. If you are primarily selling digital products, an eCommerce platform like Shopify or WooCommerce may be ideal. These platforms offer user-friendly interfaces and built-in payment processing, making it easy to set up your online store and manage inventory.

For those focused on content creation, a website built on platforms like WordPress or Squarespace can provide the flexibility to showcase your expertise through blogs, articles, and other resources. WordPress, in particular, is highly customizable and offers a vast selection of themes and plugins to enhance functionality.

If your business model revolves around courses or memberships, platforms like Teachable, Thinkific, or Kajabi offer tailored solutions for creating and selling online courses. These platforms include features such as video hosting, quizzes, and community forums, allowing you to create a comprehensive learning experience for your students.

Social media platforms, including Instagram, Facebook, and LinkedIn, are also essential components of your online presence. While they may not serve as standalone websites, they provide valuable opportunities for engagement, promotion, and community building. Integrating social media with your website can enhance your overall digital strategy.

Regardless of the platform you choose, ensure that it is mobile-friendly. With more consumers accessing the internet through mobile devices, having a responsive design is essential for providing a seamless experience. Google prioritizes mobile-friendliness in its search rankings, so this aspect can also impact your SEO efforts.

Case Study: Gymshark

Gymshark is a fitness apparel brand that has successfully leveraged various online platforms to build its brand. Starting as a small eCommerce website, Gymshark focused on selling high-quality workout gear. The brand utilized social media, particularly Instagram, to engage with fitness enthusiasts and build a community around its products.

By combining an intuitive eCommerce platform with a strong social media presence, Gymshark has grown into a multi-million dollar business. Its success illustrates the importance of choosing the right platform and effectively integrating various online channels to create a cohesive brand presence.

Essential Pages for Your Digital Business

Once you have chosen the appropriate platform, the next step is to create essential pages that will serve as the backbone of your online presence. Each page plays a crucial role in providing information, building trust, and facilitating conversions.

A homepage is the first impression visitors will have of your digital business. It should clearly convey your brand identity, values, and offerings. Consider using a clean design with engaging visuals and concise copy that communicates your unique selling proposition. Including a clear call to action (CTA) will guide visitors toward taking the next steps, whether it's exploring your products or signing up for a newsletter.

An "About" page is essential for building a personal connection with your audience. Share your story, mission, and values to help visitors understand who you are and what drives your business. People are often more inclined to support businesses with relatable and authentic stories. Include photos or videos to humanize your brand further and create a sense of familiarity.

Your "Products" or "Services" page should provide detailed information about what you offer. Include high-quality images, descriptions, and pricing for each product or service. Consider organizing your offerings into categories to make navigation easier for visitors. If you sell digital products, ensure that the purchasing process is straightforward and user-friendly.

A blog or resources page can serve as a valuable tool for establishing your authority in your niche. By creating informative and engaging content, you can attract organic traffic and provide value to your audience. Consider writing articles, guides, and tutorials that address common questions or challenges faced by your target audience. Regularly updating your blog with fresh content can also boost your SEO efforts.

A "Contact" page is crucial for facilitating communication with your audience. Provide multiple ways for visitors to reach you, whether through a contact form, email address, or social media links. Additionally, consider including a FAQ section to address common inquiries, which can save time for both you and your customers.

Finally, don't forget to include a "Privacy Policy" and "Terms of Service" page. These pages outline how you handle user data and the terms governing the use of your website. While they may not be the most exciting pages, they are essential for building trust and complying with legal requirements.

Case Study: The Skimm

The Skimm, a daily newsletter that simplifies news for busy women, has built a successful online presence through its well-structured website. The homepage effectively communicates the brand's mission, encouraging visitors to sign up for the newsletter. The "About" page shares the founders' story, helping users connect with the brand on a personal level.

The Skimm also features a blog that covers relevant topics, providing valuable insights and attracting organic traffic. By creating essential pages that resonate with its audience, The Skimm has established itself as a trusted source of information.

Optimizing for SEO

Search engine optimization (SEO) is the practice of optimizing your website to improve its visibility on search engine results pages (SERPs). A strong SEO strategy is essential for driving organic traffic to your site and increasing your brand's online presence.

The first step in optimizing for SEO is conducting keyword

research. Identify keywords and phrases that your target audience is likely to use when searching for products or information in your niche. Tools like Google Keyword Planner, SEMrush, and Ahrefs can help you uncover valuable keywords with high search volume and low competition.

Once you have identified relevant keywords, strategically incorporate them into your website content. This includes your homepage, product descriptions, blog posts, and meta tags. However, it's important to maintain a natural flow in your writing; avoid keyword stuffing, as this can harm your SEO efforts and make your content less engaging.

On-page SEO elements, such as title tags and meta descriptions, are crucial for optimizing individual pages. Your title tag should be concise and include your primary keyword, while the meta description provides a brief summary of the page's content. Both elements play a significant role in attracting clicks from search engine users.

Creating high-quality, valuable content is another critical aspect of SEO. Search engines prioritize content that provides value to users. Focus on producing informative blog posts, guides, and resources that address the needs and interests of your audience. Engaging content is more likely to be shared, linked to, and referenced by others, which can improve your search rankings.

In addition to on-page SEO, consider off-page SEO strategies, such as building backlinks. Backlinks are links from other websites that direct users to your site. High-quality backlinks from reputable sources signal to search engines that your content is valuable and trustworthy. You can build backlinks through guest blogging, collaborations, and outreach to industry influencers.

Finally, ensure that your website is technically optimized for SEO. This includes improving site speed, ensuring mobile responsiveness, and creating an XML sitemap. A well-structured website with fast loading times enhances user experience and can positively impact your search rankings.

Case Study: Moz

Moz, a well-known SEO software company, has effectively utilized SEO to establish its authority in the digital marketing space. The company's blog is filled with valuable content that addresses various aspects of SEO, attracting a significant audience. Moz employs strategic keyword optimization, engages in link-building efforts, and consistently produces high-quality content that resonates with its audience.

By focusing on SEO best practices, Moz has become a go-to resource for marketers seeking to improve their search engine rankings. Their success illustrates the importance of a well-executed SEO strategy in building an online presence.

Practical Advice for Setting Up Your Online Presence

As you embark on the journey of establishing your online presence, consider the following practical tips:

Define Your Goals: Before setting up your online presence,

clarify your business goals. What do you want to achieve with your website? Whether it's generating leads, selling products, or building brand awareness, having clear goals will guide your decisions throughout the process.

Choose the Right Domain Name: Your domain name is your online address and should reflect your brand identity. Choose a name that is memorable, easy to spell, and relevant to your business. Keep it short and avoid using complex words or phrases.

Prioritize User Experience: A user-friendly website is essential for keeping visitors engaged. Ensure that your site is easy to navigate, with clear categories and CTAs. Test your website on different devices and browsers to ensure a seamless experience for all users.

Invest in Quality Hosting: Choosing a reliable hosting provider is crucial for your website's performance. Look for a provider that offers fast loading times, good customer support, and strong security features. A slow or unreliable website can deter visitors and negatively impact your SEO efforts.

Utilize Analytics Tools: Implement analytics tools like Google Analytics to track your website's performance. Monitor key metrics such as traffic, bounce rates, and conversion rates to gain insights into user behavior. Use this data to make informed decisions and optimize your online presence.

Regularly Update Your Content: Fresh and updated content is essential for maintaining your online presence. Regularly review and update your website's content, especially your blog and product pages. This not only helps with SEO but also keeps your audience engaged and informed.

Engage with Your Audience: Building relationships with your audience is crucial for long-term success. Respond to comments, engage on social media, and encourage feedback. Creating a sense of community fosters loyalty and encourages repeat business.

Stay Informed About Trends: The digital landscape is constantly evolving, and staying informed about trends is essential. Follow industry blogs, attend webinars, and participate in online communities to stay up-to-date on best practices and emerging strategies.

Setting up your online presence is a critical step in building a successful digital marketing empire. By choosing the right platform, creating essential pages, and optimizing for SEO, you can establish a strong foundation for your business.

As you move forward, remember that your online presence is not a one-time setup but an ongoing process. Continuously engage with your audience, adapt to changing trends, and refine your strategies to maximize your impact in the digital marketplace.

In the upcoming chapters, we will explore effective marketing strategies to promote your digital products and reach your target audience, empowering you to achieve your business goals.

CHAPTER 7: Digital Marketing Strategies

IN THE DYNAMIC landscape of digital marketing, having a well-rounded strategy is essential for attracting and retaining customers. This chapter explores various digital marketing strategies, including content marketing, social media marketing, email marketing, and pay-per-click (PPC) advertising. Each of these strategies plays a significant role in promoting your brand, reaching your target audience, and driving conversions.

Content Marketing: Blogging, Videos, and Webinars

Content marketing is the practice of creating and distributing valuable content to attract and engage your target audience. It helps establish your authority, foster trust, and ultimately drive conversions. Different forms of content—such as blogging, videos, and webinars—can be employed to reach your audience effectively.

Blogging is one of the most accessible and effective forms of content marketing. Regularly publishing blog posts allows you to share your expertise, provide valuable information, and improve your website's SEO. By targeting relevant keywords and addressing common questions or pain points faced by your audience, you can attract organic traffic to your site.

When creating blog content, consider using a mix of formats, such as how-to guides, listicles, case studies, and opinion pieces. Incorporate visuals, such as images and infographics, to enhance engagement. Furthermore, promoting your blog posts through social media and email newsletters can help increase their visibility.

Video content is another powerful tool for engaging your audience. Videos can convey complex information in an easily digestible format, making them an effective way to demonstrate products, share tutorials, or tell your brand story. Platforms like YouTube, Instagram, and TikTok have made video content more accessible than ever.

When creating videos, focus on delivering value and capturing attention within the first few seconds. Invest in good equipment and editing software to ensure high production quality. Additionally, optimize your video titles, descriptions, and tags for SEO to improve discoverability.

Webinars are an excellent way to connect with your audience in real time while providing valuable information. They allow for interactive engagement, enabling participants to ask questions and participate in discussions. Webinars can be used to showcase your expertise, launch new products, or provide training.

To host a successful webinar, choose a relevant topic that

addresses your audience's needs or interests. Promote the event through social media, email campaigns, and your website. After the webinar, consider repurposing the content into blog posts or video snippets to extend its reach.

Case Study: HubSpot

HubSpot is a prime example of a company that has successfully leveraged content marketing. Through its blog, HubSpot provides valuable insights on inbound marketing, sales, and customer service. The company consistently publishes high-quality content, including guides, templates, and case studies, which has helped establish it as a leading authority in the marketing industry.

In addition to blogging, HubSpot offers webinars and video tutorials that further engage its audience. By providing valuable resources, HubSpot has built a loyal following and successfully nurtured leads, ultimately driving conversions.

Social Media Marketing: Choosing the Right Platforms

Social media marketing involves using social media platforms to connect with your audience, promote your brand, and drive traffic to your website. With numerous platforms available, it's essential to choose the right ones that align with your target audience and business goals.

To determine the best platforms for your brand, start by identifying where your target audience spends their time. For instance, if you're targeting a younger demographic, platforms like Instagram and TikTok may be more effective. On the other hand, if your audience consists of professionals, LinkedIn might be the ideal choice.

Once you've identified the right platforms, develop a content strategy tailored to each. Different platforms have unique characteristics and user expectations. For example, visual content performs well on Instagram, while informative articles and discussions thrive on LinkedIn.

Consistency is key in social media marketing. Create a content calendar to plan and schedule your posts in advance. This helps maintain a consistent posting frequency and ensures that you remain engaged with your audience. Utilize tools like Hootsuite or Buffer to streamline scheduling and monitoring.

Engagement is another crucial aspect of social media marketing. Actively respond to comments and messages, and encourage discussions within your community. Building relationships with your audience fosters loyalty and can lead to increased brand advocacy.

Additionally, consider using paid advertising on social media platforms to expand your reach. Social media ads allow you to target specific demographics, interests, and behaviors, maximizing the effectiveness of your campaigns. Experiment with different ad formats, such as carousel ads, video ads, and sponsored posts, to see what resonates best with your audience.

Case Study: Nike

Nike is a leading brand that effectively utilizes social media marketing. The company has a strong presence on various platforms, including Instagram, Twitter, and Facebook. Nike's social media strategy focuses on storytelling, showcasing inspiring athletes and promoting a lifestyle that resonates with its audience.

Through engaging content, Nike fosters a sense of community among its followers. The brand also leverages user-generated content by encouraging customers to share their experiences with Nike products. This strategy not only enhances brand loyalty but also increases visibility through authentic endorsements.

Email Marketing: Building and Nurturing Your List

Email marketing is one of the most effective digital marketing strategies for building relationships with your audience and nurturing leads. By capturing email addresses through sign-up forms or lead magnets, you can create a targeted list of subscribers interested in your offerings.

To build your email list, consider offering valuable resources in exchange for contact information. This could include e-books, checklists, webinars, or exclusive discounts. Promoting these lead magnets through your website, social media, and content marketing efforts can help drive sign-ups.

Once you have a list of subscribers, it's essential to nurture these relationships through regular communication. Develop an email marketing strategy that includes a mix of promotional content, valuable resources, and personalized messages. Segment your email list based on interests or behaviors to ensure that your messages resonate with specific groups.

Creating engaging and compelling email content is crucial for maintaining subscriber interest. Use attention-grabbing subject lines to encourage opens, and focus on providing value in the body of the email. Incorporate visuals, such as images and GIFs, to enhance engagement.

Automation is a powerful feature of email marketing platforms. Utilize automation tools to send targeted emails based on user behavior or triggers. For example, you can set up welcome emails for new subscribers, follow-up emails after a purchase, or re-engagement campaigns for inactive subscribers.

Regularly analyze your email marketing metrics, including open rates, click-through rates, and conversion rates. This data will help you refine your strategy and improve the effectiveness of your campaigns over time.

Case Study: Birchbox

Birchbox, a subscription box service for beauty products, has successfully leveraged email marketing to build and nurture its customer base. The company offers personalized recommendations based on customer preferences, creating a tailored experience for subscribers.

Birchbox sends regular emails that include product information, beauty tips, and exclusive discounts. By providing valuable content and maintaining consistent communication, the company has fostered strong relationships with its subscribers, leading to increased retention and loyalty.

Pay-Per-Click Advertising: Google Ads and Social Ads

Pay-per-click (PPC) advertising is a powerful strategy for driving targeted traffic to your website. With PPC, you can create ads that appear on search engines or social media platforms, paying only when users click on your ads. This approach allows for precise targeting and immediate visibility.

Google Ads is one of the most popular PPC advertising platforms. It allows you to create ads that appear in search results when users search for specific keywords related to your business. Conduct thorough keyword research to identify relevant keywords with high search volume and low competition. Craft compelling ad copy that highlights your unique selling proposition and encourages clicks.

In addition to search ads, Google Ads also offers display ads, which appear on websites within the Google Display Network. Display ads can help raise brand awareness and retarget users who have previously visited your site. Utilize eye-catching visuals and concise messaging to capture attention.

Social media ads, such as those on Facebook, Instagram, and LinkedIn, allow for targeted advertising based on user demographics, interests, and behaviors. Create visually appealing ads that align with your brand identity and resonate with your target audience. Experiment with different ad formats, including carousel ads, video ads, and stories, to see what drives the best results.

Monitoring and optimizing your PPC campaigns is essential for maximizing ROI. Regularly analyze key metrics, such as click-through rates, conversion rates, and cost per acquisition. Adjust your bidding strategies, ad copy, and targeting based on performance data to improve campaign effectiveness.

Case Study: Airbnb

Airbnb effectively uses PPC advertising to reach potential customers. The company runs targeted Google Ads that appear when users search for accommodations in specific locations. By utilizing compelling ad copy and visually appealing images, Airbnb captures the attention of travelers looking for unique stays.

Airbnb also leverages social media advertising to promote its offerings. The company creates engaging ads that showcase beautiful properties and highlight user experiences. By targeting specific demographics and interests, Airbnb successfully drives traffic to its platform and increases bookings.

Digital marketing strategies are essential for building a successful online presence and driving conversions. By leveraging content marketing, social media marketing, email marketing, and pay-per-click advertising, you can effectively reach your target audience and foster lasting relationships.

As you implement these strategies, remember to monitor your performance and adapt your approach based on data and feedback. The digital landscape is constantly evolving, and staying informed about the latest trends and best practices will help you maximize your impact in the digital marketplace.

CHAPTER 8:
Building an Engaged Audience

In the world of digital marketing, successfully building an engaged audience is critical for long-term success. An engaged audience not only converts into customers but also becomes advocates for your brand, helping spread the word and attract new customers. This chapter will explore strategies for growing your audience, creating a community around your brand, and leveraging user-generated content (UGC) to foster deeper connections with your audience.

Strategies for Growing Your Audience

Growing your audience requires a multi-faceted approach that combines various marketing strategies and channels. Here are several effective methods to expand your reach and attract new followers.

One of the most effective ways to grow your audience is by producing high-quality, valuable content. Content marketing, as discussed in the previous chapter, is essential for attracting new visitors to your website and converting them into loyal followers. By creating valuable blog posts, videos, podcasts, or infographics that address your audience's needs and interests, you can position yourself as an authority in your niche.

Implementing search engine optimization (SEO) strategies can further enhance your content's visibility. By optimizing your content for relevant keywords, you can attract organic traffic from search engines. Additionally, sharing your content on social media and engaging with your audience can help increase its reach and promote sharing.

Another effective strategy is to collaborate with influencers or other brands in your industry. Influencer marketing has become a powerful way to reach new audiences, as influencers have established trust and credibility with their followers. Partnering with influencers who align with your brand values can help you tap into their audience and gain exposure to potential customers.

Consider hosting giveaways or contests to create excitement and attract new followers. Encourage participants to share your content or tag friends for entries, expanding your reach and increasing engagement. This strategy not only helps grow your audience but also fosters a sense of community and connection.

Email marketing is another powerful tool for audience growth. By offering valuable resources or exclusive content in exchange for email sign-ups, you can build a targeted list of subscribers interested in your offerings. Regularly sending out newsletters with valuable content and updates keeps your audience engaged and encourages them to share your information with others.

Lastly, consider utilizing paid advertising to accelerate audience growth. Platforms like Facebook, Instagram, and Google Ads allow you to target specific demographics and interests, ensuring your ads reach the right audience. Experiment with different ad formats and messaging to determine what resonates best with your target market.

Case Study: Glossier

Glossier, a beauty brand known for its skincare and makeup products, has effectively utilized social media and influencer marketing to grow its audience. The company launched with a strong emphasis on community engagement, encouraging customers to share their experiences and feedback.

By collaborating with beauty influencers and leveraging user-generated content, Glossier has built a loyal following. The brand actively engages with its audience on platforms like Instagram, where it features real customers using its products. This strategy not only enhances brand visibility but also fosters a sense of connection and community among its followers.

Creating a Community Around Your Brand

Building a community around your brand goes beyond simply acquiring followers; it involves fostering meaningful connections and relationships with your audience. A strong community creates loyalty, encourages repeat business, and drives word-of-mouth referrals.

One effective way to create a community is by establishing a dedicated online space where your audience can interact and engage with one another. This could take the form of a Facebook group, a forum on your website, or a community on platforms like Discord or Slack. These spaces encourage discussions, allow members to ask questions, and provide a sense of belonging.

Hosting events, both online and offline, can also strengthen community ties. Consider organizing webinars, workshops, or live Q&A sessions where your audience can connect with you and each other. These events provide opportunities for learning and engagement, allowing members to share experiences and insights.

Encouraging participation and feedback is vital for fostering an engaged community. Actively solicit input from your audience on product development, content ideas, or brand initiatives. This not only makes your audience feel valued but also gives them a sense of ownership in your brand's journey.

Creating exclusive content or perks for community members can further enhance their experience. Consider offering members access to behind-the-scenes content, early product releases, or exclusive discounts. These incentives can boost engagement and encourage members to remain active participants in your community.

Regularly engaging with your audience is crucial for building strong relationships. Respond to comments, answer questions, and acknowledge contributions in your community spaces. This interaction fosters a sense of connection and shows that you genuinely care about your audience.

Case Study: Peloton

Peloton, a fitness brand known for its stationary bikes and online workout classes, has successfully built a strong community around its products. The company encourages members to engage with one another through its app and social media platforms.

Peloton hosts live classes where users can interact in real time, cheering each other on and sharing their progress. The brand also features user testimonials and success stories, creating a sense of camaraderie among members. This community-driven approach has turned Peloton users into dedicated advocates who actively promote the brand to others.

Leveraging User-Generated Content

User-generated content (UGC) refers to any content created by your customers or audience that showcases their experiences with your brand. UGC can take many forms, including photos, videos, testimonials, and reviews. Leveraging UGC can amplify your marketing efforts, build trust, and enhance engagement with your audience.

One of the most effective ways to encourage UGC is by creating campaigns that invite customers to share their experiences. For example, consider creating a branded hashtag that customers can use when posting about your products on social media. This not only encourages sharing but also allows you to easily track and showcase user-generated content.

Feature UGC on your website and social media channels to highlight real customers using your products. This not only adds authenticity but also serves as social proof, reassuring potential customers about the quality and value of your offerings. Consider creating dedicated sections on your website to showcase customer testimonials or a gallery of user-submitted photos.

Engaging with users who share content about your brand is essential. Acknowledge and thank customers for their contributions, and consider offering incentives such as discounts or recognition for those who actively participate. This fosters a sense of community and encourages more users to share their experiences.

Incorporating UGC into your marketing campaigns can also enhance engagement. For instance, you could create social media ads that feature user-generated content, showcasing real customers enjoying your products. This authentic representation can resonate more with potential customers than traditional advertising.

Moreover, UGC can provide valuable insights into how your audience perceives your brand and products. Analyzing UGC can help you identify trends, preferences, and areas for improvement. This feedback can inform your product development and marketing strategies.

Case Study: Starbucks

Starbucks is a great example of a brand that effectively leverages user-generated content. The company encourages customers to share their coffee experiences using the hashtag #Starbucks on social media. By promoting this hashtag, Starbucks has created a vast collection of user-generated content that showcases its products.

Starbucks actively features UGC on its social media channels, highlighting real customers enjoying their beverages. This not only fosters a sense of community but also encourages more customers to share their experiences, further amplifying the brand's reach.

The company also runs campaigns that encourage customers to share their Starbucks stories, allowing for authentic engagement and connection. By leveraging UGC, Starbucks has built a loyal and engaged audience that actively promotes the brand.

Practical Advice for Building an Engaged Audience

As you work to build an engaged audience, consider the following practical tips:

Be Authentic: Authenticity is key in building trust with your audience. Be genuine in your communication, and share your brand's story, values, and experiences. Authenticity fosters connections and encourages engagement.

Encourage Feedback: Actively solicit feedback from your audience and show that you value their opinions. Implementing their suggestions demonstrates that you listen and care, leading to increased loyalty and engagement.

Create Shareable Content: Develop content that encourages sharing, whether it's informative blog posts, entertaining videos, or visually appealing graphics. Shareable content can help extend your reach and attract new followers.

Utilize Engagement Tools: Use polls, surveys, and quizzes to engage your audience and encourage participation. These tools can help you gather insights while making your audience feel involved.

Regularly Interact: Engage with your audience consistently. Respond to comments, answer questions, and acknowledge contributions. Regular interaction fosters a sense of community and connection.

Monitor Metrics: Keep track of relevant metrics to gauge audience engagement. Analyze social media interactions, email open rates, and website traffic to identify trends and opportunities for improvement.

Stay Consistent: Consistency in messaging, branding, and engagement is crucial. Maintain a regular posting schedule and ensure that your communications align with your brand values and voice.

Building an engaged audience is essential for the long-term success of your digital marketing efforts. By implementing strategies for growing your audience, creating a community around your brand, and leveraging user-generated content, you can foster meaningful connections with your audience.

As you continue to engage with your audience, remember that building a community is an ongoing process. Stay authentic, encourage participation, and consistently deliver value.

CHAPTER 9:
Monetization Strategies

MONETIZING YOUR DIGITAL products effectively is crucial for sustaining and growing your business. This chapter will explore various monetization strategies, including pricing your digital products, employing upselling and cross-selling techniques, and leveraging affiliate marketing opportunities. By understanding and implementing these strategies, you can maximize your revenue potential and create a thriving digital marketing empire.

Pricing Your Digital Products

Setting the right price for your digital products is a vital aspect of your monetization strategy. The price you choose affects not only your revenue but also your perceived value in the market. Here are several factors to consider when pricing your digital products.

First, conduct market research to understand the pricing

landscape for similar products in your niche. Analyze your competitors and see what they charge for their offerings. This will give you an idea of the market rate and help you position your products competitively. However, don't just mimic their pricing; consider how your product stands out and the unique value it provides.

Next, consider your target audience's willingness to pay. Understanding your audience's demographics, preferences, and pain points can help you gauge how much they might be willing to invest in your products. Surveys and polls can be effective tools for gathering insights into your audience's pricing expectations.

When setting a price, also factor in your production costs and desired profit margins. Ensure that your pricing covers the costs associated with creating and delivering your digital products while allowing for a reasonable profit. For example, if you're selling an online course, consider the time and resources spent on content creation, platform fees, and marketing expenses.

Another strategy is to adopt tiered pricing. Offering multiple pricing options allows you to cater to different customer segments. For instance, you could offer a basic version of your product at a lower price, while providing a premium version with additional features or benefits at a higher price point. This approach not only maximizes your revenue potential but also ensures that customers can choose the option that best suits their needs and budget.

Additionally, consider implementing psychological pricing strategies. For example, pricing your product at \$29.99 instead of \$30 can create the perception of a better deal. Similarly, using "charm pricing" (ending prices with .99 or .95) can evoke a sense of value and encourage purchases.

Finally, be open to adjusting your prices over time. As your business grows and your products evolve, you may find that your pricing needs to be reevaluated. Monitor customer feedback, sales performance, and market trends to determine when and how to adjust your pricing strategy.

Case Study: Udemy

Udemy, an online learning platform, has effectively utilized tiered pricing strategies for its courses. Instructors set their own prices, typically ranging from $19.99 to $199.99, depending on the course content and value. Udemy also frequently offers discounts and promotions, creating a sense of urgency and incentivizing purchases.

By analyzing customer behavior and preferences, Udemy has optimized its pricing strategy, offering both affordable and premium courses. This approach has helped the platform grow significantly, attracting millions of learners worldwide while generating substantial revenue for course creators.

Upselling and Cross-Selling Techniques

Upselling and cross-selling are powerful monetization techniques that can significantly increase your average order value. Both strategies focus on encouraging customers to spend more by offering complementary or enhanced products.

Upselling involves persuading customers to purchase a more expensive version of the product they are considering. For example, if a customer is interested in buying a basic online course, you might present them with an upgraded version that includes additional modules, one-on-one coaching, or exclusive resources. The key to successful upselling is to clearly communicate the added value of the upgraded product.

To implement effective upselling, consider the following strategies:

1. **Highlight Benefits:** Clearly articulate the benefits of the upgraded product. Use persuasive language to demonstrate how the additional features will enhance the customer's experience or help them achieve their goals more effectively.
2. **Use Visuals:** Incorporate visuals, such as comparison charts or images, to help customers visualize the differences between the basic and upgraded versions. This can make the upsell more compelling.
3. **Timing is Key:** Present upsell options at the right moment, such as during the checkout process or after the customer has made their initial purchase. This timing can increase the likelihood of conversion.

Cross-selling, on the other hand, involves recommending related products that complement the customer's original purchase. For example, if a customer buys an e-book on digital marketing, you could suggest a related online course or a toolkit of templates that would enhance their learning experience.

To effectively cross-sell, consider the following techniques:

4. **Personalized Recommendations:** Use customer data and behavior to provide personalized product recommendations. This could include suggesting products based on previous purchases or items frequently bought together.
5. **Bundles and Packages:** Create product bundles that offer a discount when customers purchase multiple related items together. This not only encourages additional purchases but also provides perceived value to the customer.
6. **Follow-Up Emails:** After a purchase, send follow-up emails featuring related products. This keeps your brand top-of-mind and encourages customers to explore additional offerings.
7. **On-Site Recommendations:** Incorporate cross-selling prompts on your website. For example, on the product page, you can display "Customers who bought this also bought…" to encourage further exploration.

Case Study: Amazon

Amazon is a master of upselling and cross-selling techniques. The platform uses personalized recommendations based on user behavior, showcasing related products and encouraging customers to explore additional items.

For instance, when a customer adds a product to their cart,

Amazon often suggests complementary items, such as accessories or related products. This strategy has proven highly effective, contributing significantly to Amazon's revenue growth and making it a leader in e-commerce.

Affiliate Marketing Opportunities

Affiliate marketing is a performance-based marketing strategy that allows you to earn commissions by promoting other companies' products or services. This approach can be an excellent way to monetize your audience while providing them with valuable recommendations.

To get started with affiliate marketing, consider the following steps:

1. **Choose the Right Affiliate Programs**: Identify affiliate programs that align with your niche and audience interests. Look for reputable companies with products or services that you genuinely believe will benefit your audience. Popular affiliate programs include Amazon Associates, ShareASale, and CJ Affiliate.
2. **Create Quality Content**: Develop content that integrates affiliate products naturally. This could include product reviews, tutorials, or blog posts that highlight how the products solve specific problems. Be transparent about your affiliate relationships, as this builds trust with your audience.

3. **Use Tracking Links:** Most affiliate programs provide unique tracking links that monitor clicks and conversions. Use these links in your content to ensure you receive credit for any sales generated through your promotions.
4. **Leverage Email Marketing:** Incorporate affiliate promotions into your email marketing campaigns. Send targeted emails featuring affiliate products that align with your audience's interests. Ensure the messaging is genuine and focuses on providing value.
5. **Promote on Social Media:** Use your social media platforms to share affiliate products. Create engaging posts, stories, or videos that highlight the benefits of the products while including your affiliate links.
6. **Analyze Performance:** Regularly monitor the performance of your affiliate marketing efforts. Track which products generate the most clicks and conversions, and adjust your strategies accordingly. This will help you optimize your affiliate marketing approach for better results.

Case Study: Pat Flynn

Pat Flynn, a well-known entrepreneur and author, has effectively leveraged affiliate marketing to generate income through his website, Smart Passive Income. Flynn shares valuable insights and resources related to online business and marketing, integrating affiliate products that align with his audience's interests.

By providing genuine reviews and recommendations for

products he uses and trusts, Flynn has built a loyal following. His transparency and authenticity have contributed to his success in affiliate marketing, helping him earn significant income while providing value to his audience.

Practical Advice for Monetization Strategies

As you explore various monetization strategies, consider the following practical tips:

Understand Your Audience: Knowing your audience's preferences and pain points is crucial for effective monetization. Conduct surveys, gather feedback, and analyze customer behavior to tailor your strategies to their needs.

Test and Iterate: Don't be afraid to experiment with different pricing models, upselling techniques, or affiliate programs. Monitor the results and make adjustments based on performance data to optimize your strategies.

Provide Value First: Always prioritize providing value to your audience. Whether through high-quality content, exceptional customer service, or genuine recommendations, focusing on their needs will foster trust and loyalty.

Use Analytics: Utilize analytics tools to track the performance of your monetization efforts. Understanding metrics such as conversion rates, average order value, and customer lifetime value will help you make informed decisions.

Stay Adaptable: The digital landscape is constantly evolving. Stay informed about industry trends and be willing to adapt your strategies as needed. This flexibility will help you remain competitive and maximize your revenue potential.

Monetization strategies are essential for building a sustainable and profitable digital marketing empire. By effectively pricing your digital products, employing upselling and cross-selling techniques, and leveraging affiliate marketing opportunities, you can maximize your revenue potential and create a thriving business.

As you implement these strategies, remember to prioritize your audience's needs and provide value at every step.

CHAPTER 10: Scaling Your Business

Scaling your business is a critical step toward achieving long-term growth and sustainability in the digital marketplace. As your business expands, it's essential to implement strategies that allow you to manage increased demand without compromising quality or customer satisfaction. This chapter will explore key strategies for scaling your business, including automating your marketing efforts, outsourcing and building a team, and expanding your product line. By understanding and applying these strategies, you can set your business up for success in the digital landscape.

Automating Your Marketing Efforts

Marketing automation refers to the use of technology to streamline and automate repetitive marketing tasks. This approach allows you to focus on high-level strategy and creative tasks while ensuring that your marketing efforts run smoothly and efficiently. Here are several ways to automate your marketing efforts effectively.

1. **Email Marketing Automation:** Email marketing is a cornerstone of digital marketing, and automating your campaigns can save you time while improving engagement. Use platforms like Mailchimp, ActiveCampaign, or ConvertKit to set up automated email sequences. For example, you can create a welcome series for new subscribers that introduces them to your brand, shares valuable resources, and promotes your products. Additionally, consider setting up triggered emails that send based on user behavior, such as abandoned cart reminders or post-purchase follow-ups.
2. **Social Media Scheduling:** Consistent social media presence is vital for engaging your audience, but manually posting can be time-consuming. Use scheduling tools like Buffer, Hootsuite, or Later to plan and automate your social media posts. This allows you to maintain a consistent posting schedule and engage with your audience without the daily time commitment. Additionally, you can analyze the performance of your posts to refine your strategy.
3. **Lead Generation and Nurturing:** Automating lead generation processes can help you capture and nurture potential customers more effectively. Use landing page builders like Leadpages or Unbounce to create optimized lead capture pages. Integrate these pages with your email

marketing platform to automatically add new subscribers to your lists. Implement lead scoring to prioritize and segment leads based on their engagement levels, allowing you to tailor your follow-up strategy.

4. **Customer Relationship Management (CRM) Systems:** Implementing a CRM system can help you manage customer interactions and streamline communications. Platforms like HubSpot, Salesforce, or Zoho CRM allow you to track customer data, interactions, and sales processes. Automate follow-up reminders, task assignments, and customer segmentation to enhance your sales and marketing efforts.
5. **Analytics and Reporting:** Automating data collection and reporting can save you time and provide valuable insights into your marketing performance. Use tools like Google Analytics, SEMrush, or Sprout Social to monitor key performance indicators (KPIs) automatically. Set up custom dashboards that provide real-time insights into your marketing efforts, enabling you to make informed decisions based on data.
6. **Chatbots and Customer Support Automation:** Implementing chatbots on your website can enhance customer support and engagement. Chatbots can answer frequently asked questions, guide users through the purchase process, and capture leads outside of regular business hours. Tools like Drift and Intercom offer

user-friendly chatbot solutions that can be integrated into your website.

Case Study: HubSpot

HubSpot is a prime example of a company that has effectively utilized marketing automation to scale its business. The platform offers a comprehensive suite of marketing, sales, and customer service tools that allow businesses to automate various marketing tasks. HubSpot's marketing automation capabilities include email marketing workflows, social media scheduling, and lead nurturing sequences.

By automating these processes, HubSpot has been able to efficiently manage its operations while providing valuable resources to its customers. The company's commitment to automation has contributed to its growth, making it a leading player in the inbound marketing space.

Outsourcing and Building a Team

As your business scales, you may find that you cannot handle all tasks alone. Outsourcing specific functions and building a team can help you focus on higher-level strategies while ensuring that essential tasks are completed efficiently. Here are some key considerations for outsourcing and building a successful team.

1. **Identify Core Competencies:** Begin by identifying the core competencies of your business and the areas where you require assistance. This could include marketing,

content creation, customer support, graphic design, or website development. Understanding your strengths and weaknesses will help you determine which tasks to outsource.

2. **Hire Freelancers or Agencies**: For specific tasks, consider hiring freelancers or agencies. Platforms like Upwork, Fiverr, and Freelancer offer access to a wide range of professionals who can assist with various projects. For instance, you might hire a freelance graphic designer to create marketing materials or an agency to manage your social media accounts.
3. **Build an In-House Team**: As your business grows, you may want to build an in-house team for more complex functions. Hiring employees allows for greater control over processes and fosters collaboration. Consider hiring individuals with complementary skills, such as a content marketer, social media manager, or customer support representative.
4. **Utilize Virtual Assistants (VAs)**: Virtual assistants can be an excellent resource for managing administrative tasks. They can handle a variety of functions, such as email management, scheduling, data entry, and customer support. Hiring a VA can free up your time to focus on more strategic aspects of your business.
5. **Establish Clear Communication**: As you build your team, effective communication is essential for collaboration and

productivity. Utilize tools like Slack, Asana, or Trello to facilitate communication and project management. Set clear expectations, deadlines, and performance metrics to ensure everyone is aligned and accountable.

6. **Foster a Positive Company Culture**: Creating a positive company culture is vital for retaining talent and fostering collaboration. Encourage open communication, provide opportunities for professional development, and recognize team members' contributions. A supportive work environment enhances job satisfaction and productivity.
7. **Regularly Evaluate Performance**: Continuously assess the performance of your team and outsourced functions. Set up regular check-ins and performance reviews to identify areas for improvement. Encourage feedback from team members and address any issues promptly to maintain a positive and productive work environment.

Case Study: Buffer

Buffer, a social media management platform, has effectively scaled its business by outsourcing and building a remote team. The company has embraced a remote work culture, allowing it to hire talent from around the world. Buffer utilizes various tools to facilitate communication and collaboration among its team members.

By outsourcing specific functions, such as content creation and customer support, Buffer has been able to focus on product development and strategic initiatives. The company's commitment to building a positive remote work culture has contributed to its growth and success in the competitive social media landscape.

Expanding Your Product Line

Expanding your product line is a strategic approach to scaling your business and increasing revenue. By offering a diverse range of products, you can cater to different audience segments and meet varying customer needs. Here are some key strategies for expanding your product line effectively.

1. **Conduct Market Research**: Before expanding your product line, conduct thorough market research to identify opportunities and gaps in the market. Analyze customer feedback, industry trends, and competitor offerings to determine which products would resonate with your audience.
2. **Leverage Customer Feedback**: Engage with your existing customers to gather insights into their needs and preferences. Consider conducting surveys, interviews, or focus groups to understand what additional products they would find valuable. This feedback can guide your product development efforts.
3. **Develop Complementary Products**: When expanding your product line, consider creating complementary products that enhance your existing offerings. For example, if you sell online courses, consider offering

related resources like workbooks, templates, or coaching services. This approach encourages existing customers to purchase additional items while providing more value.

4. **Test New Products**: Before fully launching new products, consider conducting a soft launch or pilot program. This allows you to gather feedback and assess demand before investing heavily in production and marketing. Use this opportunity to fine-tune your offerings based on customer responses.
5. **Diversify Your Offerings**: Explore different product formats to diversify your offerings. For example, if you primarily sell e-books, consider creating video courses, podcasts, or membership programs. This variety can attract new customers and cater to different learning preferences.
6. **Create Subscription Models**: Subscription models provide a steady stream of recurring revenue while delivering ongoing value to customers. Consider offering subscription services for digital products, such as monthly access to exclusive content, courses, or resources. This approach fosters customer loyalty and encourages long-term engagement.
7. **Implement Bundling Strategies**: Bundling products can increase sales by offering customers perceived value. Create packages that combine related products at a

discounted price. This encourages customers to purchase multiple items while enhancing their overall experience.

8. **Monitor Market Trends**: Stay informed about industry trends and emerging technologies that may influence your product offerings. Regularly assess market dynamics and adjust your product line to remain competitive. This adaptability will help you capitalize on new opportunities as they arise.

Practical Advice for Scaling Your Business

As you explore strategies for scaling your business, consider the following practical tips:

1. **Set Clear Goals**: Define your scaling objectives and establish measurable goals. Whether it's increasing revenue, expanding your customer base, or launching new products, having clear goals will help guide your efforts and keep you focused.
2. **Prioritize Efficiency**: Look for ways to streamline processes and eliminate inefficiencies. Regularly assess your workflows and identify areas for improvement. Efficiency is key to managing increased demand without sacrificing quality.
3. **Embrace Technology**: Leverage technology and tools to enhance productivity and automate repetitive tasks. Invest in software solutions that align with your business needs and facilitate collaboration among team members.

4. **Focus on Customer Experience:** As you scale, prioritize providing exceptional customer experiences. Ensure that your products, services, and support meet or exceed customer expectations. Happy customers are more likely to become repeat buyers and advocates for your brand.
5. **Build Strong Relationships:** Foster relationships with your customers and team members. Regularly communicate and engage with your audience to build trust and loyalty. A strong community enhances your brand and drives long-term success.
6. **Stay Adaptable:** The digital landscape is continually evolving. Be open to adapting your strategies and processes as needed. Stay informed about industry trends and emerging technologies that may impact your business.
7. **Monitor Financial Health:** As your business scales, keep a close eye on your financial health. Regularly review your cash flow, expenses, and profit margins to ensure sustainability. Invest wisely in growth opportunities while maintaining a solid financial foundation.
8. **Celebrate Milestones:** Scaling a business is a journey, and it's essential to celebrate milestones along the way. Acknowledge the achievements of your team and recognize the hard work that has contributed to your success. Celebrating milestones fosters motivation and camaraderie.

Scaling your business is a crucial step toward achieving

long-term growth and success in the digital marketplace. By automating your marketing efforts, outsourcing and building a team, and expanding your product line, you can effectively manage increased demand while maintaining quality.

As you implement these strategies, remember to prioritize efficiency, customer experience, and adaptability. The journey of scaling your business requires careful planning and execution, but with the right approach, you can build a thriving digital marketing empire.

CHAPTER 11: Measuring Success

IN THE DYNAMIC world of digital marketing, measuring success is paramount to understanding the effectiveness of your strategies and making informed decisions for future growth. This chapter will delve into the importance of tracking key performance indicators (KPIs), analyzing data to derive actionable insights, and adapting and evolving your strategies based on performance metrics. By mastering these elements, you can ensure that your digital marketing efforts are optimized for success.

Tracking Key Performance Indicators (KPIs)

Key Performance Indicators (KPIs) are quantifiable metrics that help you evaluate the success of your marketing efforts in relation to your business objectives. By tracking KPIs, you can gain insights into how well your strategies are performing and identify areas for improvement. Here are some essential KPIs to consider for your digital marketing efforts:

1. **Website Traffic**: Tracking the number of visitors to your website is fundamental for understanding your overall reach. Use tools like Google Analytics to monitor total visits, unique visitors, and page views. Analyzing traffic sources can help you identify which channels (organic search, social media, email, etc.) are driving the most visitors.

2. **Conversion Rate**: The conversion rate measures the percentage of visitors who complete a desired action on your website, such as making a purchase, signing up for a newsletter, or filling out a contact form. To calculate the conversion rate, divide the number of conversions by the total number of visitors and multiply by 100. A high conversion rate indicates that your marketing efforts are effectively persuading visitors to take action.
3. **Customer Acquisition Cost (CAC)**: CAC measures the cost associated with acquiring a new customer. To calculate CAC, divide your total marketing expenses by the number of new customers acquired during a specific period. Understanding CAC helps you assess the efficiency of your marketing strategies and budget allocation.
4. **Customer Lifetime Value (CLV)**: CLV estimates the total revenue a customer is expected to generate over their entire relationship with your business. To calculate CLV, multiply the average purchase value, purchase frequency, and average customer lifespan. Comparing

CLV with CAC can help you assess the profitability of your marketing efforts.

5. **Return on Investment (ROI):** ROI measures the profitability of your marketing campaigns. To calculate ROI, subtract the total cost of the campaign from the total revenue generated, divide by the total cost, and multiply by 100. A positive ROI indicates that your marketing efforts are generating more revenue than they cost.
6. **Engagement Metrics:** Monitoring engagement metrics, such as likes, shares, comments, and click-through rates (CTR), provides insights into how well your content resonates with your audience. High engagement rates indicate that your audience finds your content valuable and relevant.
7. **Email Open and Click Rates:** For email marketing campaigns, tracking open rates (the percentage of recipients who open your email) and click rates (the percentage of recipients who click on links within your email) is essential. These metrics help you gauge the effectiveness of your subject lines and content, allowing you to optimize future campaigns.

Case Study: HubSpot

HubSpot, a leading inbound marketing platform, effectively utilizes KPIs to measure the success of its marketing efforts. By tracking various metrics, including website traffic, conversion rates, and customer acquisition costs, HubSpot gains valuable insights into the performance of its campaigns.

For example, HubSpot regularly analyzes its conversion rates from landing pages and employs A/B testing to optimize these pages. By measuring the impact of different headlines, images, and calls to action, the company continuously improves its conversion rates and overall marketing effectiveness.

Analyzing Data to Make Informed Decisions

Data analysis plays a crucial role in informing your marketing decisions and optimizing your strategies. By collecting and interpreting data, you can identify trends, understand customer behavior, and make data-driven choices that enhance your marketing efforts. Here are some key steps to effectively analyze data:

1. **Collect Data Systematically**: Establish a systematic approach to data collection. Use analytics tools like Google Analytics, social media insights, and email marketing platforms to gather relevant data. Ensure that you have proper tracking mechanisms in place, such as UTM parameters for links, to attribute conversions accurately.
2. **Segment Your Data**: Segmenting your data allows you to analyze specific subsets of your audience or campaigns. For example, you can segment data by demographics, geographic location, or traffic source. This granular analysis helps identify patterns and trends within specific

groups, enabling you to tailor your marketing strategies accordingly.

3. **Identify Trends and Patterns:** Look for trends and patterns in your data over time. For instance, if you notice a consistent increase in website traffic during specific months or after launching particular campaigns, it may be indicative of successful marketing efforts. Identifying these trends can guide your decision-making and help you capitalize on successful strategies.
4. **Use Visualization Tools:** Data visualization tools, such as Google Data Studio or Tableau, can help you present complex data in a visually appealing and easy-to-understand format. Visualizing data through charts, graphs, and dashboards allows you to quickly identify trends and make informed decisions based on clear insights.
5. **Conduct A/B Testing:** A/B testing involves comparing two versions of a marketing asset (e.g., a landing page, email, or ad) to determine which performs better. By systematically testing different elements, such as headlines, images, or calls to action, you can identify the most effective strategies and optimize your campaigns accordingly.
6. **Monitor Competitor Performance:** Keeping an eye on your competitors can provide valuable insights into industry trends and best practices. Use tools like SEMrush or Ahrefs to analyze competitor performance, including their website traffic, keyword rankings, and

social media engagement. Understanding what works for your competitors can inform your strategies and help you stay competitive.

7. **Implement Feedback Loops:** Establish feedback loops to continuously gather insights from your audience. Encourage customer feedback through surveys, reviews, and social media interactions. Analyze this feedback to identify areas for improvement and adapt your marketing strategies based on customer preferences.

Case Study: Netflix

Netflix is known for its data-driven approach to decision-making. The company extensively analyzes viewer data to gain insights into customer preferences and behaviors. By tracking viewing habits, such as which shows and movies are popular and at what times users are watching, Netflix can make informed decisions about content creation and marketing strategies.

For example, Netflix uses data to personalize recommendations for its users, enhancing the viewing experience and increasing engagement. The company also conducts A/B testing on its user interface to optimize user experience, ensuring that its platform remains user-friendly and appealing.

Adapting and Evolving Your Strategies

In the fast-paced world of digital marketing, adaptability is key to sustained success. As you gather data and analyze performance, it's essential to be open to change and willing to evolve your strategies based on insights and market dynamics. Here are some practical tips for adapting and evolving your marketing strategies:

1. **Stay Agile:** Cultivate an agile mindset within your team, encouraging flexibility and responsiveness to changing market conditions. Regularly review your marketing strategies and be prepared to pivot if certain tactics are not delivering the desired results.
2. **Set Regular Review Cycles:** Establish regular review cycles to assess the performance of your marketing campaigns and strategies. Schedule monthly, quarterly, or biannual assessments to analyze KPIs and make data-driven adjustments. This structured approach ensures that you stay on track and continuously improve your marketing efforts.
3. **Incorporate Customer Feedback:** Actively seek and incorporate customer feedback into your strategies. Regularly engage with your audience through surveys, social media, and customer support interactions. Understanding their needs and preferences allows you to refine your offerings and tailor your marketing messages effectively.
4. **Experiment with New Tactics:** Don't be afraid to experiment with new marketing tactics and platforms. For

example, if you haven't explored influencer marketing, consider collaborating with influencers in your niche to reach new audiences. Testing new approaches can uncover untapped opportunities for growth.

5. **Monitor Industry Trends:** Stay informed about industry trends and emerging technologies that may impact your marketing strategies. Subscribe to industry newsletters, follow thought leaders, and participate in webinars to keep your knowledge up-to-date. This awareness allows you to adapt proactively to changes in the marketplace.
6. **Embrace Continuous Learning:** Encourage a culture of continuous learning within your team. Invest in training and professional development opportunities to enhance your team members' skills and knowledge. Staying ahead of the curve in digital marketing trends and strategies positions your business for success.
7. **Document Your Learnings:** Keep a record of your marketing experiments, successes, and failures. Documenting your learnings allows you to build a knowledge base that informs future decision-making. Review past campaigns to identify what worked, what didn't, and why.

Case Study: Starbucks

Starbucks is known for its ability to adapt and evolve its marketing strategies in response to changing customer preferences and market trends. For instance, the company has embraced digital transformation by launching its mobile app, which allows customers to order and pay ahead of time.

Starbucks continuously analyzes customer data and feedback to refine its offerings. The company actively engages with customers on social media, responding to feedback and adjusting its product offerings based on customer preferences. By staying agile and responsive to its audience, Starbucks has maintained its position as a leader in the coffee industry.

Practical Advice for Measuring Success

To effectively measure success in your digital marketing efforts, consider the following practical tips:

1. **Define Clear Objectives:** Establish clear and measurable objectives for your marketing campaigns. Ensure that your KPIs align with these objectives to track progress effectively.
2. **Use the Right Tools:** Invest in the right analytics and reporting tools to monitor your KPIs. Ensure that you have the necessary technology to collect and analyze data efficiently.
3. **Focus on Actionable Insights:** Analyze data with the goal of deriving actionable insights. Avoid getting lost

in the numbers; instead, focus on identifying trends and patterns that inform decision-making.

4. **Be Patient and Persistent**: Measuring success is an ongoing process that requires patience and persistence. Results may not be immediate, so stay committed to tracking and analyzing your marketing efforts over time.
5. **Engage Your Team**: Involve your team in the measurement process. Encourage collaboration and open discussions about performance metrics, insights, and potential adjustments to strategies.
6. **Celebrate Wins**: Acknowledge and celebrate successes, no matter how small. Recognizing achievements boosts team morale and motivates continued effort toward achieving your marketing goals.
7. **Stay Committed to Improvement**: Embrace a mindset of continuous improvement. Regularly assess your strategies and be open to evolving your approach based on insights and changing market dynamics.

Measuring success in digital marketing is crucial for understanding the effectiveness of your strategies and making informed decisions for future growth. By tracking key performance indicators (KPIs), analyzing data to derive actionable insights, and adapting your strategies based on performance metrics, you can optimize your marketing efforts for success.

As you implement these measurement strategies, remember to stay agile, engage your audience, and continuously seek opportunities for improvement. The journey of measuring success is ongoing, and by remaining committed to data-driven decision-making, you can build a thriving digital marketing empire.

CHAPTER 12:
Overcoming Challenges

IN THE EVER-EVOLVING landscape of digital marketing, challenges are an inevitable part of the journey. Whether you're a seasoned marketer or just starting, you'll encounter obstacles that can impede your progress and test your resolve. This chapter will delve into common challenges faced in digital marketing, strategies for staying motivated and resilient, and the importance of learning from failure. By understanding these aspects, you can better navigate the complexities of digital marketing and build a thriving empire.

Common Obstacles in Digital Marketing

Digital marketing offers numerous opportunities for growth and engagement, but it also presents a range of challenges. Here are some common obstacles you may encounter:

1. **Rapidly Changing Algorithms**: Digital platforms frequently update their algorithms, affecting how content

is ranked and displayed. For instance, Google updates its search algorithms regularly to enhance user experience. As a result, businesses must stay informed and adapt their SEO strategies to maintain visibility in search results. This can be particularly challenging for small businesses that may lack the resources to keep up with these changes.

2. **Information Overload**: The sheer volume of content produced daily can make it difficult for marketers to stand out. With millions of blogs, videos, and social media posts competing for attention, crafting content that resonates with your target audience is crucial. Developing a unique voice and perspective is essential in a crowded digital landscape.
3. **Customer Trust and Privacy Concerns**: With growing concerns over data privacy and security, consumers are becoming increasingly cautious about sharing their information. Businesses must navigate these concerns while still effectively reaching their audience. Building trust through transparency, ethical data practices, and clear communication is essential for overcoming this obstacle.
4. **Budget Constraints**: Many businesses face budget constraints that limit their marketing capabilities. Small businesses, in particular, may struggle to allocate sufficient funds for advertising, content creation, and technology. This challenge requires creative solutions,

such as leveraging organic marketing strategies and utilizing cost-effective tools.

5. **Ad Fatigue:** Consumers are bombarded with advertisements across multiple channels, leading to ad fatigue. This phenomenon occurs when users become desensitized to marketing messages, resulting in decreased engagement and conversion rates. To combat ad fatigue, marketers need to focus on delivering relevant and valuable content rather than relying solely on promotional messages.
6. **Measuring ROI:** Demonstrating the return on investment (ROI) for digital marketing efforts can be challenging. With multiple channels and touchpoints, attributing conversions to specific campaigns requires careful tracking and analysis. Businesses need to implement robust measurement systems to evaluate the effectiveness of their marketing strategies.
7. **Maintaining Consistency:** Consistency is key to building a strong brand presence, but it can be difficult to maintain across various platforms and channels. Inconsistent messaging and branding can confuse customers and weaken brand identity. Developing a cohesive content strategy and ensuring alignment across all marketing efforts is essential.

Case Study: Airbnb

Airbnb faced significant challenges as it scaled its business. One of the most pressing obstacles was navigating regulatory issues in various markets. As the company expanded globally, it encountered local laws and regulations that affected its operations. For example, in cities like New York and San Francisco, short-term rental regulations posed hurdles for hosts and the platform alike.

To overcome this challenge, Airbnb adopted a proactive approach by engaging with local governments and stakeholders. The company initiated partnerships with city officials, advocating for sensible regulations that balanced community interests with the needs of hosts and guests. By addressing regulatory challenges head-on, Airbnb was able to sustain its growth while building trust with local communities.

How to Stay Motivated and Resilient

Facing challenges in digital marketing can be disheartening, but maintaining motivation and resilience is vital for long-term success. Here are some strategies to help you stay focused and motivated:

1. **Set Clear Goals**: Establishing clear, achievable goals provides direction and purpose. Break down larger objectives into smaller, manageable milestones, allowing you to track progress and celebrate small wins along the way.

This sense of accomplishment can boost motivation and keep you engaged.

2. **Embrace a Growth Mindset**: Adopting a growth mindset—believing that abilities and intelligence can be developed—can help you navigate challenges with resilience. Embrace setbacks as opportunities for learning and growth rather than as failures. This perspective fosters curiosity and encourages you to seek solutions rather than dwell on problems.
3. **Surround Yourself with Support**: Building a network of like-minded individuals can provide encouragement and support during challenging times. Join online communities, attend industry events, or connect with mentors who can offer guidance and share their experiences. Having a supportive network can help you stay motivated and inspired.
4. **Practice Self-Care**: Taking care of your physical and mental well-being is essential for maintaining motivation. Prioritize self-care practices, such as exercise, mindfulness, and adequate rest. These habits can help reduce stress and enhance your overall resilience, allowing you to tackle challenges with a clearer mindset.
5. **Stay Informed and Educated**: The digital marketing landscape is continuously evolving, and staying informed about industry trends and best practices can keep you motivated. Attend webinars, read industry blogs, and

participate in online courses to enhance your knowledge and skills. Continuous learning can reignite your passion and provide fresh perspectives on overcoming challenges.

6. **Celebrate Achievements**: Take the time to celebrate your achievements, both big and small. Acknowledging your progress reinforces your motivation and reminds you of the hard work you've put in. Consider keeping a success journal where you document your accomplishments and positive feedback from customers or peers.
7. **Adapt and Adjust**: Flexibility is essential in navigating challenges. When faced with setbacks, be willing to adapt your strategies or pivot your approach. Embracing change and being open to new ideas can help you find innovative solutions to overcome obstacles.

Case Study: Nike

Nike is a prime example of a company that has maintained motivation and resilience in the face of challenges. The brand has navigated various obstacles, including economic downturns, changing consumer preferences, and intense competition.

During the COVID-19 pandemic, Nike faced significant disruptions to its supply chain and retail operations. Instead of succumbing to the challenges, Nike quickly pivoted its strategy to focus on digital transformation. The brand accelerated its e-commerce efforts, launched virtual workout experiences, and engaged with customers through social media.

By embracing innovation and adapting to changing circumstances, Nike not only survived the challenges but also strengthened its brand presence. The company's resilience and commitment to staying connected with its audience allowed it to thrive in a challenging environment.

Learning from Failure

Failure is an inevitable part of any business journey, and embracing it as a learning opportunity can lead to growth and improvement. Here are some strategies for learning from failure:

1. **Analyze the Situation**: When faced with failure, take the time to analyze what went wrong. Identify specific factors that contributed to the unsuccessful outcome. Consider whether it was a result of poor planning, lack of resources, or external circumstances. Understanding the root cause is essential for preventing similar issues in the future.
2. **Seek Feedback**: Gathering feedback from team members, customers, or mentors can provide valuable insights into your failures. Encourage open and honest discussions about what could have been done differently. This feedback can help you identify blind spots and inform your future strategies.
3. **Document Lessons Learned**: Keep a record of your failures and the lessons learned from each experience. Documenting these insights can serve as a reference for future decision-making. Reflecting on past challenges can

provide valuable guidance and prevent you from repeating the same mistakes.

4. **Embrace a Culture of Experimentation**: Encourage a culture of experimentation within your team. Foster an environment where trying new ideas and approaches is welcomed, even if it leads to failure. Emphasize that failure is a natural part of the learning process and can lead to innovative solutions.
5. **Focus on Solutions**: Instead of dwelling on the failure itself, shift your focus to potential solutions. Brainstorm ways to overcome the challenges you faced and develop a plan for improvement. This proactive approach can help you regain momentum and confidence.
6. **Be Kind to Yourself**: It's easy to be critical of yourself after a setback, but practicing self-compassion is crucial. Recognize that everyone experiences failure, and it's a normal part of the journey. Treat yourself with kindness and use the experience as an opportunity for growth.

Case Study: Starbucks

Starbucks encountered challenges when it attempted to expand its product line beyond coffee. The company launched the "Starbucks Music" initiative, which aimed to sell music and create an in-store experience around music. However, the venture failed to gain traction and was eventually discontinued.

Instead of viewing this failure as a setback, Starbucks used it as a learning opportunity. The company analyzed the reasons behind the failure, including a lack of consumer interest and competition from established music platforms. By gathering insights from this experience, Starbucks refocused its efforts on enhancing its core offerings and improving the customer experience.

This commitment to learning from failure has allowed Starbucks to maintain its position as a leader in the coffee industry. The company continuously innovates while remaining true to its brand identity, ensuring that it meets customer expectations.

Practical Advice for Overcoming Challenges

As you navigate the challenges of digital marketing, consider the following practical tips:

1. **Embrace Change:** Change is a constant in digital marketing. Be open to adapting your strategies and evolving your approach as needed. Staying flexible will help you respond effectively to challenges.
2. **Develop a Problem-Solving Mindset:** Cultivate a mindset focused on finding solutions rather than dwelling on obstacles. When faced with challenges, ask yourself, "What can I do to overcome this?" This proactive approach will empower you to take action.
3. **Build Resilience:** Resilience is a skill that can be developed over time. Practice self-care, seek support, and prioritize your well-being to strengthen your ability to bounce back from setbacks.

4. **Stay Committed to Your Vision**: Remind yourself of your long-term goals and vision for your business. Staying committed to your purpose will help you stay motivated during challenging times.
5. **Learn from Others**: Seek inspiration from others who have faced similar challenges. Read case studies, attend industry events, and engage with thought leaders to gain insights into how they overcame obstacles.
6. **Maintain a Positive Attitude**: A positive attitude can significantly impact your ability to navigate challenges. Focus on what you can control and maintain an optimistic outlook even in difficult situations.
7. **Seek Professional Development**: Invest in your skills and knowledge through training, workshops, and courses. Continuous learning will equip you with the tools needed to overcome challenges effectively.
8. **Reflect and Adjust**: Regularly reflect on your experiences and assess your strategies. Be willing to adjust your approach based on insights gained from challenges and failures.

Overcoming challenges is an integral part of the digital marketing journey. By recognizing common obstacles, staying motivated and resilient, and learning from failure, you can navigate the complexities of digital marketing with confidence.

As you implement these strategies, remember that challenges are opportunities for growth and improvement. Embrace change, cultivate a problem-solving mindset, and stay committed to your vision.

CHAPTER 13:
Future Trends in Digital Marketing

As the digital marketing landscape continues to evolve, staying ahead of emerging trends is essential for businesses looking to thrive in a competitive environment. This chapter will explore future trends in digital marketing, focusing on emerging technologies and their impact, the shift towards personalization, and the growing importance of sustainability. By understanding these trends, you can position your business for success in the ever-changing digital landscape.

Emerging Technologies and Their Impact

Emerging technologies are revolutionizing the way businesses engage with their customers and conduct marketing activities. Here are several key technologies shaping the future of digital marketing:

1. **Artificial Intelligence (AI)**: AI is one of the most transformative technologies in digital marketing. It enables

businesses to analyze vast amounts of data quickly and derive actionable insights. AI-powered tools can automate tasks such as customer segmentation, content generation, and predictive analytics. For instance, chatbots powered by AI can provide instant customer support, enhancing user experiences while reducing operational costs.*Example*: Companies like Drift and Intercom are leveraging AI to create chatbots that engage visitors on websites, answer common questions, and guide users through the sales funnel. This not only improves customer satisfaction but also allows businesses to gather valuable data on customer interactions.

2. **Voice Search and Smart Speakers**: The rise of voice-activated devices like Amazon Alexa, Google Assistant, and Apple Siri is changing how consumers search for information. Voice search queries tend to be more conversational and longer than traditional text searches, prompting businesses to optimize their content accordingly. Marketers must focus on natural language processing (NLP) and keyword strategies that cater to voice search. *Example*: A local restaurant could optimize its website for voice search by using questions and answers relevant to common queries, such as "What are the best Italian restaurants near me?" This optimization can improve visibility in voice search results, driving more foot traffic to the establishment.

3. **Augmented Reality (AR) and Virtual Reality (VR)**: AR and VR technologies are transforming how brands engage customers by providing immersive experiences. These technologies enable consumers to visualize products in their own environments before making a purchase decision. For example, furniture retailers can use AR applications to allow customers to see how a piece of furniture would look in their home.*Example*: IKEA's AR app, IKEA Place, allows users to visualize furniture in their living spaces before purchasing. This interactive experience not only enhances customer engagement but also reduces the likelihood of returns, as customers can make more informed decisions.
4. **Blockchain Technology**: Blockchain technology has significant implications for digital marketing, particularly in enhancing transparency and trust. By securely recording transactions and data, blockchain can help combat issues such as ad fraud and data breaches. Brands can leverage blockchain to provide consumers with verifiable information about product sourcing and authenticity.*Example*: The luxury fashion brand Everledger uses blockchain to track the provenance of diamonds and other luxury goods. By providing a transparent supply chain, Everledger helps consumers make informed purchasing decisions and combats the issue of counterfeit products.
5. **5G Technology**: The rollout of 5G networks is set to revolutionize mobile marketing by providing faster

internet speeds and more reliable connections. This technology will enable richer content experiences, such as high-definition video streaming and advanced mobile applications. Marketers can leverage 5G to create more engaging and interactive campaigns. *Example*: With 5G technology, brands can create augmented reality experiences that require high bandwidth. For instance, a car manufacturer could offer an AR app that allows customers to virtually test drive vehicles in real-time, enhancing the overall customer experience.

6. **Internet of Things (IoT)**: The IoT refers to the interconnected network of devices that communicate with each other. Marketers can leverage IoT data to gain insights into consumer behavior and preferences. For example, smart home devices can provide valuable data on customer usage patterns, enabling brands to tailor their offerings more effectively. *Example*: Nest, a smart thermostat company, collects data on how users interact with their devices. This data helps Nest improve its products and offers personalized recommendations to users based on their energy usage habits.

The Shift Towards Personalization

Personalization has become a key focus for marketers as consumers increasingly expect tailored experiences. The shift towards personalization is driven by advancements in data analytics and AI, allowing businesses to deliver relevant content and offers to individual customers. Here are some strategies for leveraging personalization in digital marketing:

7. **Data-Driven Insights**: Collecting and analyzing customer data is crucial for understanding preferences and behavior. Utilize tools like Google Analytics, CRM systems, and social media insights to gather data on customer demographics, interests, and interactions. This information can help you create targeted marketing campaigns that resonate with your audience.*Example*: Netflix uses data analytics to understand viewer preferences and recommend content based on individual viewing habits. By analyzing user behavior, Netflix can personalize recommendations, increasing viewer engagement and retention.
8. **Dynamic Content**: Implementing dynamic content on your website or in email marketing allows you to tailor experiences based on user behavior. For example, displaying different product recommendations based on previous purchases or browsing history can enhance the user experience and drive conversions.*Example*: Amazon is known for its personalized product recommendations, displaying items based on customers' browsing and purchase history. This dynamic approach encourages customers to explore additional products and increases the likelihood of repeat purchases.

9. **Segmentation**: Segmenting your audience based on specific criteria—such as demographics, behavior, or interests—enables you to deliver more relevant content and offers. Tailored messaging can significantly improve engagement and conversion rates.*Example*: A fitness brand might segment its audience into groups based on fitness goals (e.g., weight loss, muscle gain, endurance). By sending targeted email campaigns that address the specific needs of each segment, the brand can increase the relevance of its messaging and improve overall engagement.
10. **Personalized Email Marketing**: Email marketing remains a powerful tool for personalization. Use customer data to customize email content, subject lines, and offers based on individual preferences. Personalized emails have been shown to generate higher open and click-through rates.

    Example: Spotify sends personalized playlists and recommendations to users based on their listening history, creating a tailored experience that keeps users engaged and encourages retention.
11. **Behavioral Targeting**: Utilize behavioral targeting techniques to reach customers based on their online actions. By analyzing user behavior, you can deliver relevant ads and content to potential customers at the right time.

    Example: Retargeting ads allow brands to display ads to

users who have previously visited their website but did not complete a purchase. By reminding users of products they showed interest in, brands can encourage them to return and complete the transaction.

12. **Customer Journeys**: Mapping customer journeys provides insights into the various touchpoints and interactions customers have with your brand. Understanding these journeys allows you to create personalized experiences at each stage, from awareness to conversion.

    Example: A travel company might identify various touchpoints in a customer's journey, such as searching for destinations, booking flights, and sharing travel experiences. By personalizing content at each stage, the company can enhance customer engagement and satisfaction.

Sustainability in Digital Marketing

As consumers become more environmentally conscious, sustainability is emerging as a critical trend in digital marketing. Brands that prioritize sustainability in their marketing strategies can build trust and loyalty among eco-conscious consumers. Here are some ways to incorporate sustainability into your digital marketing efforts:

13. **Transparent Communication**: Clearly communicate your sustainability initiatives and practices. Consumers appreciate transparency and want to understand how brands are making a positive impact on the environment.

Share information about sourcing, production processes, and efforts to reduce carbon footprints.

Example: The outdoor clothing brand Patagonia is known for its commitment to environmental sustainability. The company openly shares its environmental initiatives, such as using recycled materials and promoting responsible consumption, reinforcing its brand values and building consumer trust.

14. **Eco-Friendly Messaging:** Incorporate eco-friendly messaging into your marketing campaigns. Highlight sustainable practices, products, and initiatives in your advertising to resonate with environmentally conscious consumers.

    Example: Unilever's "Sustainable Living" campaign promotes its commitment to sustainability, emphasizing eco-friendly products and practices. By aligning its marketing messages with sustainability, Unilever appeals to consumers who prioritize environmental responsibility.

15. **Sustainable Packaging:** Consider implementing sustainable packaging solutions for your products. Eco-friendly packaging not only reduces environmental impact but also enhances your brand's reputation among consumers who value sustainability.

    Example: Coca-Cola has committed to using 100% recyclable packaging by 2025. By focusing on sustainable packaging, the company aims to reduce waste and promote environmental consciousness among its customers.

16. **Partnerships with NGOs**: Collaborate with non-governmental organizations (NGOs) or environmental groups to support sustainable initiatives. Highlighting these partnerships in your marketing efforts can demonstrate your commitment to social responsibility.

    Example: TOMS Shoes has a well-known partnership with various NGOs to provide shoes to children in need. The company's "One for One" model emphasizes social impact, attracting consumers who value brands that contribute to positive change.

17. **Sustainable Content Creation**: Create content that educates and informs consumers about sustainability issues. By sharing valuable information, you can position your brand as a thought leader in the sustainability space and engage consumers on important topics.

    Example: National Geographic produces content that raises awareness about environmental issues and promotes sustainable practices. By aligning its brand with sustainability, National Geographic engages consumers who are passionate about the environment.

18. **Carbon Offsetting**: Consider implementing carbon offset programs to counterbalance your company's carbon emissions. Communicating these efforts in your marketing can resonate with consumers who prioritize sustainability.

    Example: The airline industry has seen a rise in carbon offset programs, where companies allow customers to contribute to projects that reduce carbon emissions. By offering these options, airlines can appeal to environmentally conscious travelers.

Practical Advice for Navigating Future Trends

As you prepare for the future of digital marketing, consider the following practical tips:

1. **Stay Informed**: Regularly monitor industry news, trends, and emerging technologies. Subscribe to industry publications, attend webinars, and participate in conferences to stay updated on the latest developments.
2. **Invest in Technology**: Embrace emerging technologies that align with your marketing goals. Invest in AI tools, data analytics platforms, and automation solutions to streamline processes and enhance customer experiences.
3. **Focus on Personalization**: Prioritize personalization in your marketing efforts. Leverage data to understand customer preferences and deliver tailored experiences that resonate with your audience.
4. **Embrace Sustainability**: Integrate sustainability into your brand's values and marketing strategies. Communicate your commitment to environmental responsibility and engage consumers on sustainability issues.
5. **Experiment and Innovate**: Don't be afraid to experiment with new marketing strategies and technologies. Testing

new approaches can uncover valuable insights and drive innovation within your organization.

6. **Engage with Your Audience:** Foster open communication with your audience. Encourage feedback, respond to inquiries, and engage with customers on social media to build strong relationships.
7. **Measure and Analyze:** Continuously measure the effectiveness of your marketing efforts. Use analytics tools to track performance metrics and make data-driven decisions to optimize your strategies.
8. **Be Adaptable:** The digital marketing landscape is constantly changing. Stay agile and be prepared to adapt your strategies based on emerging trends and consumer preferences.

The future of digital marketing is shaped by emerging technologies, the shift towards personalization, and the growing importance of sustainability. By understanding these trends and adapting your strategies accordingly, you can position your business for success in the evolving digital landscape.

As you navigate the future of digital marketing, remember to stay informed, embrace innovation, and prioritize customer engagement. By leveraging emerging technologies and focusing on personalized and sustainable practices, you can build a thriving digital marketing empire that resonates with consumers and drives long-term success.

ABOUT THE AUTHOR:
Angela Dodson

Angela is a dynamic marketing professional with a unique blend of expertise in marketing and psychology. Armed with a Bachelor's degree in Marketing and Psychology and a Master's degree in Marketing and Global Communications, she has spent years honing her skills in the fast-paced world of marketing. Angela's journey began as a university student, where she developed a deep understanding of consumer behavior and strategic marketing principles.

Extensive hands-on experience in various marketing roles, combined with her academic background, has equipped Angela with the tools and insights needed to navigate the complexities of modern marketing. With a passion for helping businesses thrive in the digital landscape, Angela launched her own successful digital marketing business, where she has empowered countless clients to elevate their brands and achieve their goals.

As a thought leader in the industry, Angela is dedicated to

sharing her knowledge and expertise through her writing. She believes in the transformative power of effective marketing strategies and is committed to helping others build their own digital marketing empires. When she's not working with clients or writing, Angela enjoys exploring new marketing trends, conducting research, and mentoring aspiring marketers.